THE COMPLETE
SHORT
GAME

THE COMPLETE
SHORT
GAME

The Ultimate Guide to Building and Perfecting Your
Chipping, Pitching, Putting, and Bunker Play

from two-time US Open Winner

ERNIE ELS

Broadway Books
NEW YORK

BROADWAY

Library of Congress Cataloging-in-Publication Data

Els, Ernie.
    The complete short game : the ultimate guide to building and perfecting your chipping, pitching, putting, and bunker play skills from Ernie Els. -- 1st ed.
        p. cm.
    Previous ed. : London : Collins Willow, 1998.
    Includes index.
    ISBN: 0-7679-0253-X (hardcover)
    1. Short game (Golf)   I. Title.
GV979.S54E57 1998
796.352'3--dc21   97-42435
                                                        CIP

FIRST EDITION

Designed by Cooling Brown (*Book Production*), England

98 99 00 01 02 10 9 8 7 6 5 4 3 2 1

Also by Ernie Els
How to Build a Classic Golf Swing

CONTENTS

FOREWORD

ALTHOUGH TOURNAMENT PROS hit the ball a long way, both off the tee and with the irons, the biggest difference between most amateurs and professionals lies in the short game. In fact, the closer the ball is to the green, the wider the gap is between those of us who play golf for a living and those of you who play it for fun.

This surprises a lot of people. They see someone like me – and I'm probably a good example because I'm a big hitter – and they think I make all my scores through power. That's where they're wrong. Sure, a good, solid long-game is essential. And I admit it certainly helps being able to hit long drives. But around the greens is where the score is made. I can shoot 70 one day and 66 the next and you know what, the quality of my golf from inside 100 yards is probably the only real difference. That's absolutely true, believe me.

As I say, the club golfer simply doesn't appreciate this. And it's a crying shame, because anyone can develop a good short game. I mean, there are no physical restrictions. Anyone can chip the ball, anyone can putt, anyone can play a bunker shot. You don't need muscle, you don't need flexibility and you don't need youth. You don't even need nerves of steel – at least, not all the time.

It's all down to how well you understand the techniques – and to be honest, they're not that complicated for most short shots – and how often you commit yourself to practising these shots. I know you haven't got as much time as someone like me, but you'd be amazed at the effect just one hour's worth of short-game practice a week would make to your scores. And I mean amazed. Within two months I reckon a typical mid-handicap golfer could knock two or three shots off their average score – minimum. And that has to be worth the effort.

In the following pages I'm going to cover all the shots you need to know from 100 yards and in to help you build an all-round, complete short game. A short game where you have no real weaknesses – no Achilles heel to find you out on the 18th in a competition. And remember, just an hour or two a week – that's all you need to make a huge difference to the sharpness of your short game.

ERNIE ELS

PERFECT PITCHING

'Whether it's poor technique, poor thinking, or both, the bottom line is this: If you're missing many greens with your short irons you're in real trouble. You'll have a birdie-drought for sure. Worse still, you'll be scrambling to make pars and bogeys all day, and that gets tiresome.'

PITCHING IS ONE PART of the game where the problems of a typical amateur are as much to do with attitude as they are technique. And this all comes down to expectation. Put me in a half-decent lie from anywhere under 100-yards and I'm looking to get up and down in two. In fact, not just looking, actually expecting.

Most amateurs don't see it like that. Hitting it anywhere on the green is often the extent of their ambitions. And to me, that's part of their problem. If the expectations are low, chances are the results will be, too.

That's all very well for me to say, but high expectations stem from a sound technique and I don't see a lot of that at club level. In my experience, there is a serious lack of understanding about how to play a pitch shot. That leads to a bad set-up and, 99 times out of 100, a bad swing is just around the corner.

Problems with pitching are easily solved, though. If you can grasp just a handful of principles, all the other pieces will slot into place. And once your technique is up to scratch, your mental approach will be, too. So work with me through this chapter on approach play and you'll soon be thinking not just about hitting the green, but about actually getting up and down in two shots. Just like the pros.

You have to visualise to realise

Seeing a good shot in your mind's eye is the first step to actually hitting a good shot. I really believe that if you skip this part of the pre-shot routine, your game will suffer.

So take time to build a picture of the shot you want to hit. First establish what sort of trajectory is best suited to the conditions. Wind speed and direction is obviously an important consideration, but there are other factors. For instance, if the flag is at the back of a long green, a high-floating shot probably isn't the best call. You'll stand a far better chance of hitting the ball closer to the hole if you play a lower-flighted pitch shot, one that releases a little on landing. So choose a club accordingly – a choked-down 9-iron might be a better option than a regular wedge shot.

You also need to be aware of the safe option. If there's a tricky pin position, make a decision where not to miss the green. For instance, if I'm looking at a pin that is cut tight to a bunker on the right-hand side of the green, I make doubly sure I don't let the shot leak too far right. If I did, then the chances are I'd have a tough job getting up and

Next time you watch a tournament, notice how many professionals go through a pre-shot routine of visualising the flight of the ball before moving in to take up the final address position.

down in two for my par. And dropped shots get expensive in my game. So I'll make sure I favour the left side, if anything – in other words, the fat part of the green.

Mental mistakes won't cost you much money, if any at all, but they'll hurt all the same. The pre-shot routine is there to help you avoid that. Visualising your shots before you address the ball will mean you make smarter decisions. It will help free your mind of any doubts or second-thoughts. So once you're over the ball you can concentrate 100% on the shot.

And it needn't mean slow play, either. You'll learn to think about these options as you approach your ball. When you are there, you'll be able to weigh up the options in an instant and make smarter decisions in the blink of an eye.

The regular pitch shot

SET-UP FOR SHOW...

One of the most common misconceptions when it comes to pitching is that you need an open stance to begin with. But, as I say, it is just that – a misconception. The reality is that if you stand way open at address, it inevitably leads to more hand action and not enough body action during the swing – the sort of imbalance that's bound to create problems.

You can have your feet open the merest fraction, but that's all. Your shoulders and whole upper body must be square to the target line. This is important, so every time you get the chance, have a friend check your body alignment for you. It should ensure you don't drift into any bad habits.

As for the other elements of a good set-up, obviously correct posture is essential. The angles you create at address will influence the shape of your swing, so make sure they are the correct angles. Feel like you bend from the hips – sticking out your backside should do the trick – and flex your knees just a touch. Not too much, though, or your weight

My right shoulder is over the outside of my right knee, confirming that I'm standing the correct distance from the ball

will have a tendency to rock back towards your heels. That's definitely not what you want. What you should actually feel is that your weight is over the balls of your feet.

Finally with regard to your set-up, check that your ball position is three ball's-widths inside your left heel. That's far enough back to encourage a descending angle of attack and crisp, ball-turf contact, but not so far back that you get too steep on it. Be strict with yourself on this one – it's important.

QUICK POSTURE CHECK

In good posture, your right shoulder should be over a point between the outside of your right knee-cap and your right toes, your spine should be fairly straight and there should be a comfortable amount of flex in your knees. To achieve this during a practice session, perform this quick and easy drill.

Stand upright, holding the shaft of a club against the top of your thighs like you would a weight lifter's bar-bell (left). Now bend very slowly from the waist, sticking out your backside a little and flexing your knees at the same time. As you do this, apply pressure with the shaft of the club on to the top of your thighs, almost as though you're pushing the shaft down against the resistance created by the muscles in your legs. Now you're in good shape. Simply flip the club into its normal position and without changing a thing, except to relax a little, proceed as if to hit a shot (right).

Now if you were to perform this in front of mirror, as though you're about to hit directly away from it, you'll notice when you glance back that a vertical line drawn down from your shoulder would intersect with your toes. A small gap either side is acceptable.

In the backswing keep your lower half solid and maintain the flex in your knees thus building resistance in your swing.

...AND SWING FOR DOUGH

A lot of golfers at club level fail to appreciate one of the beauties of the golf swing, namely that a fundamentally correct set-up actually promotes a good swing. There are no maybes here, that's fact. So for all of you who took the time to read through the previous page...congratulations, you're already on the way to becoming a better pitcher of the ball. And we've hardly started, yet!

So a good set-up encourages a good golf swing. But you still need to be aware of the elements that make up a successful pitching action. I like to think of it as a blend between arm-swing and body rotation.

In the backswing I sense that I keep my lower half pretty solid, maintaining the flex in my knees and not letting my hips 'give' too much. This enables me to wind-up my upper body more effectively in the backswing, creating the resistance which helps fire a more dynamic downswing. It's just like when you wind up a spring – the harder you wind it, the faster it unwinds.

And that's basically what happens in the downswing. I unwind my upper body and sense that I really zip the clubhead through impact with a positive hand and arm swing. I feel that there's freedom in my swing as I flow through impact to a balanced finish.

All of this creates a nice, crisp strike, ball then divot. The ball is loaded with backspin and that means lots of control – the name of the game when it comes to the short game.

One final thing, never force a pitch shot. Know your range and stick to it – that's certainly what I do. My perfect distance for the club I'm using here, the 56-degree sand-wedge, is 95 yards. If it's any more than that to the flag, or if there's a stiff breeze in my face, then I take more club. It's as simple as that.

Please bear in mind, though, these are all reference points. The golf swing is not a game of dot-to-dot and you can't attempt to join together each of these positions, hoping they'll add up to the perfect golf swing. It doesn't work like that. The golf swing is a movement, it's something that should flow.

Breaking it down and analysing it in this way does serve several purposes, though. It allows you to identify your own mistakes and therefore correct them. It gives you something constructive to work on – it adds purpose to your practice. And that can only be a good thing. I guess this message applies right through the pages of this book.

In the downswing, unwind your upper body and combine that with a positive hand and arm swing.

Free-wheel through impact to a balanced finish.

DRILL: *Swing around the clock to control length*

The closer you get to the green, the less of a problem accuracy becomes and the more emphasis there is on judgement of distance. By that I mean you're not going to hit too many chip shots or pitch shots miles off line, but you are likely to leave plenty either a long way short or a long way past. That's the case with virtually every shot from 100 yards in.

On that basis, then, the first step towards a better short game is having a greater sense of control over how far the ball flies through the air. To achieve that you need a system whereby you can judge distance at least fairly accurately. I don't expect you to get as good as the pros – we have all day to work on it – but there's absolutely no reason why you shouldn't get to the stage where very few of your pitch shots finish more than, say, 20 feet short or beyond the flag.

Give the following system a try. It's not only very simple, but very effective too. Take one club, your favourite pitching club for example, and adopt your address position. Imagine the golf ball is at 6 o'clock, with your head at 12 o'clock. Now play three shots. In the first swing, stop your hands at 9 o'clock. In the middle swing, stop them at 10 o'clock and for the longest swing 11 o'clock. Then hit a dozen shots from each hour, feeling that you accelerate the club smoothly down and through impact. Don't use unnatural acceleration, keep your rhythm and tempo constant.

9 o'clock swing

Now pace out the average distance for each of the three clockface swings and make a note of the results. You might find your performance with, say a pitching-wedge, reads something like this:

9 o'clock swing	*60 yards*
10 o'clock swing	*75 yards*
11 o'clock swing	*90 yards*

Judging distance by matching your swing-length to the hour on a clockface is a great mental image to take with you on to the golf course. So if you get the chance to rehearse these swings in front of a mirror at home, you'll speed up the learning process. You could even get someone to video you at the driving range and play it back through the view-finder so that you can match-up what you feel with what you actually do.

TIP: *GET SOME GRIP ON THE BALL*

Let me give you a little equipment advice that's pretty important throughout your game, but especially so with short iron shots. Every now and then take a wooden tee-peg and really give those grooves in the face of your wedge a good cleaning out. That gives you maximum grip on the ball and therefore maximum backspin and control. And talking of control, don't even attempt high-spin golf shots unless you play a high-spin golf ball — preferably one that has a balata cover. They are constructed in a way that enables you to create lots of backspin. Other golf balls simply do not give you that option, so if you play a two-piece golf ball don't expect to stop your pitch shots quickly on anything other than soft, receptive greens.

10 o'clock swing

11 o'clock swing

When you want to add spin…

Played correctly, a cleanly struck pitch shot usually has more than enough backspin on it. I say usually, but not always. Sometimes, most likely when the pin is cut tight to a bunker at the front of a green, you need to really make the ball sit down quickly or even screw back. That's time to play the 'pitch with fizz'.

I have already discussed the relationship between your hand and arm swing and your body motion in the regular pitch. The way you blend these two elements enables you to play different type pitch shots. The set-up stays pretty much the same, except I might place the ball just a fraction further back in my stance, but the swing should feel a little different. I'll explain exactly why.

Put simply, the high-spinning pitch shot requires more of a body-release action. Having made a regular backswing, I then really focus on unwinding my upper body in double-quick time. My rhythm stays smooth – and this is important – but there's a

Unwind your body a little more briskly in the downswing and really rip the clubhead into the ball.

definite feeling of my body rotating hard through impact. The hands and arms are not quite so active and I feel like they stay closer to my body as I zip that clubhead down and through the ball, taking a big divot – the classic sign of a descending blow and really crisp, ball-then-turf contact. There's lots of backspin in this shot, I promise you.

This all adds up to a much flatter finish position. Just look at how the shaft angle is horizontal to the ground as I swing the club into the followthrough.

This advice must be tempered with a few words of warning. It's tempting to want to make the ball dance all over the green, loaded with backspin, but it's not the easiest shot to judge and therefore it isn't what I'd call the percentage shot. For that reason I'd say to you play this shot only when you really have to – basically when there's no other effective option. But when you do decide to play it, be positive and commit yourself 110% to the shot. You need to get that set-up absolutely spot-on, then keep your swing thoughts crystal clear. Just think of really unwinding your body in the downswing and keeping your arms close to your body as you fizz the clubhead through the hitting zone.

As you accelerate the club down and through impact, sense that your arms stay close to your body.

…and when you want to take spin away

Considering how easy and effective it is, the shot I'm about to show you may well be the single most under-used pitch shot in golf. It makes the ball fly lower and spin less, which means it is super-effective when the flag is at the back of a long green. Or when the green slopes severely from front to back. Or on a links course when you want to run the ball into the green. Or when there's a stiff breeze in your face. I could go on, but I'm sure you've got the message – this is an extremely versatile shot.

If anything this is easier to play than a regular pitch shot. The first thing you need to do is take comfortably more club. If say you're going to play this shot from 90 yards, then I suggest you go with a 9-iron rather than your wedge. Set up pretty much as you would for a normal pitch shot, only narrow your stance just a fraction. Also choke down on the club roughly one inch.

Remember with the high-spinning pitch shot it was very much body orientated? This is the opposite. You need to make what feels like a real 'armsy' swing. Make a decent turn but don't let your hands get above shoulder high in the backswing and feel that

Make what feels like an 'armsy' swing and sense that your wrists don't hinge
as much as they would in a regular pitch shot.

there's definitely not as much wrist action as there would be in a normal swing. In the downswing, accelerate the club freely through impact, again keeping your wrists out of the action. This shot is virtually all arms.

What'll happen is your angle of attack will be not nearly as steep as usual, so you'll sweep the ball away, with virtually no divot at all. Also look at the difference in my followthrough, compared to the high-spinning pitch shots. You can see the evidence of more arm-swing in the way the shaft travels through on a much more upright angle, pointing to 12 o'clock as I swing through to a finish.

The ball will fly flatter than a normal pitch shot. When it lands, it will bounce forwards a couple of times, then grab a little, killing off the speed. It really is a lovely shot to pull out of the bag. And like I say, it's so very versatile you can play it in a huge variety of situations. Give it a try next time you're at the practice range – I think you'll like it a lot.

Pitching from rough

HOW DOES YOUR GRASS GROW?

We all miss fairways, but how many of us actually practise hitting shots from the rough? I know I do, but I bet there aren't too many of you reading this who can answer 'yes' to that question. I know it's tough finding time just to hit balls at all, let alone get on to the course and practise your rough play. But that needn't stop you getting better results from the rough. Providing you're familiar with the necessary mental and physical adjustments – and frankly there aren't many of those – then even just a couple of minutes hitting balls from the rough will have you controlling these shots better than you ever imagined.

First job is to check which way the grass is growing. It sounds trivial, but it's anything but that. If the grass is growing towards your target, you've got a potential flier-lie. In these situations the ball can come out very 'hot', by that I mean with very little spin. So it tends to not only fly further through the air, it also runs further, too. So you need to go down a club, maybe two, and aim to land the ball well short of the green and let it run on from there. At least you can play this one like a regular iron shot, though.

That isn't the case if the grass is growing against you – in other words, away from the target. Now you have a much tougher shot. First of all you're going to get much more interference from the grass around the ball, so you need to be very aggressive and give it a good thump. Grass growing against you makes it that much more difficult to generate distance, so in these situations it's often best to take, say, a 9-iron where a wedge might have been more than enough from the same distance out on the fairway. You also need to know your limitations. If the lie is a truly awful one, it really is best to bite the bullet and simply accept that the smartest thing to do is get the ball back in play and hope for a chip-and-putt.

BALL BACK AND THUMP IT OUT

From anything other than a flier-lie, you have to make a conscious effort in the rough to put the ball at least one ball's-width further back in your stance to help promote a steeper angle of attack into impact. Also choke down on the grip, because by shortening the effective length of the shaft you further steepen the angle of attack. In rough that's the single most important thing. One final thought for your set-up: Grip the club extra-tightly in

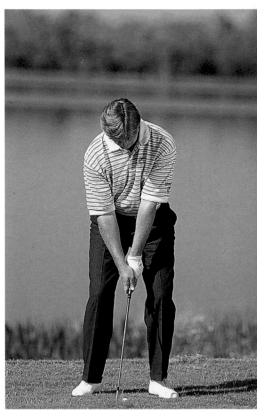

Choke down on the grip.

the bottom three fingers of your left hand. This should prevent the club twisting in your hands as it comes into contact with the thick grass around the ball.

By making those few simple changes to your address position, you've effectively pre-set a few of the necessary changes to your swing. You don't actually have to consciously adapt or manipulate your swing to any huge degree. What you do have to do, though, is be aggressive. This ball isn't going to come out of a lie like this without some serious encouragement! And that means you have to give it a good old-fashioned thump.

In the backswing keep your weight more evenly distributed than you would for a normal full iron shot – you don't want to feel like you're moving too much in to your right side. Then, as I've said, you have to be very aggressive in the downswing. Hit down as hard as you like, almost into the top of the golf ball, and rip out enough grass to make a salad for two! And swing through the ball – don't stop on it.

And just look how much grass comes out with the ball when I play this shot from a horrible lie. This impact position is the sort of image you want to conjure up in your mind as you prepare to play a shot from thick rough. It'll encourage you to put that bit of extra effort in at impact — and that's half the battle.

Always remember that rule about which way the grass is growing and learn to read how the ball is going to react. It's a simple formula: Grass growing with you, club down and allow for a flier; grass growing against you, take plenty of club and give it a thump.

Keep your weight evenly distributed, hit down extra hard, and make sure you swing through the ball.

DRILL: *Training the correct chain reaction*

Look at this mini-sequence and you'll see a very important stage of the golf swing played out stage by stage for you in perfect detail. The pictures show the transition from backswing to downswing – some say the most important split-second in the swing – and how an effective lower-body action helps set the club in the perfect position from which to attack the ball on the ideal angle of attack, which in the case of a shot from rough is a pretty steep one.

You can see how I've wound-up my shoulders and upper body in the backswing, my hips and legs resisting that turning motion. All pretty straightforward so far. But look what happens in the change of direction – that's the crucial part. See how my hips go first, travelling a long way while the club has barely moved into the downswing. It's this

As I complete the backswing I'm fully wound up. My shoulders are turned 90-degrees and I can feel my hips resisting.

'lag' effect – the lower half initiating the downswing and the hands, arms, club and upper body following – that creates the absolute perfect path and angle of attack into the ball. And there's a lot of power in there, too, because everything is happening in the correct sequence with the body-weight always moving to support the swinging motion.

Grab yourself a club and try to rehearse this all important chain reaction. Swing to the top, pause for a second, then feel your hips go first, unwinding as your knees retain their original flex well into the downswing. Can you feel how easily and naturally the club sort of slots into position – it's automatic. And from halfway down you can really give the club a good swish through impact. That's the recipe for a positive swing and a good, free release of the club.

Now my hips trigger the downswing. As I unwind my upper body
the club drops into the perfect downswing 'slot'.

The full pitch shot from sand

PICK A WEDGE AND TRUST YOUR SWING

OK, it's major dilemma time. You've got 90, maybe 100 yards to the flag. And the ball's in the sand. It's a good lie, but that's probably not enough to exactly fill you with enthusiasm or confidence. In fact, the chances are you're dreading it the moment you set eyes on a shot like this. Well that's not surprising. This is a tough shot by anyone's standards and knocking it inside, say, six feet is an exceptionally tall order. I do think any golfer should be able to find the putting surface, though. So here's how.

Adopt a slightly open stance and choke down on your grip.

This is too far from the flag to be thinking about a sand-wedge, so straight away reach for your pitching-wedge. Now adopt a slightly open stance – not too much, but enough so that a line drawn along your toes would point roughly 30 feet left of the flag. Position the ball just as you would for a normal pitch shot, roughly three ball's-widths inside your left heel. Finally, shorten the club by choking down on the grip at least two inches.

Sand is the most unforgiving surface you can play off and the strike needs to be precise, or you'll come up well short of the target. As I don't want to upset my rhythm and, more importantly, my chances of hitting the ball clean, I make a conscious effort to feel that my hips and legs stay pretty still, which keeps my swing nice and compact. That's good, you don't ever want to make more than a three-quarter swing on a shot like this – it just makes clean ball-striking too difficult.

A shallow angle of attack works best on a long pitch from sand. Here's a great tip to help you achieve that – keep your right heel in the sand for as long as possible into your downswing. That doesn't mean hang back on your right side though. You should still feel your weight drift towards the target in harmony with the swinging clubhead. But you want a definite feeling of your right heel staying in the sand until impact. This promotes the necessary shallow angle of attack, allows a greater margin for error in the hitting area, and enables you to clip the ball away cleanly.

Also, don't get flicky with your hands and wrists at impact – that's a killer. Trust the loft on the club to generate the perfect ball-flight. There might be the merest puff of sand after impact, but it shouldn't be much. If you do take a lot of sand, you're swinging too steeply for a shot like this. Try again, and remember, keep your right heel firmly planted in the sand until you feel the impact of clubhead on ball. You'll get it eventually.

Make a tidy backswing and a silky-smooth change of direction.

Feel that your right heel stays planted until you've released the club through the ball.

Ball in a divot

Look at this – typical, eh! You hit a great drive down the centre of the fairway and your ball finishes in an old divot mark. Believe me, I know what it feels like. When I won the US Open in 1994, I was on the final hole in regulation play and hit my second shot out of a terrible spot in the rough, on to the fairway, and into a horrible divot mark. Out of the frying pan, into the fire!

Your initial thoughts in this sort of situation are usually despair. The majority of club golfers I know would then hit the panic button. That's the wrong kind of attitude, though. I've learnt from experience that you have to stay calm, think the shot through in your head and then just go ahead and play it as best you can. There's no sense dwelling on your bad luck and getting yourself down. That does no good at all. Back in '94 at Oakmont I remember thinking I'd made a pretty decent job of hitting the green, from where I two-putted to make the playoff and went on to win. This isn't an easy shot but, providing the divot-mark isn't ridiculously deep, you should be able to make the green.

What you must do is put the ball further back in your stance than you have for any other shot you've ever played. In fact, probably nearer your right foot than your left. It will feel weird at first, but trust me it's the only way to go. Also, 'bump' your weight a

Keep your weight over the ball at the top of your backswing and retain the
angles in your wrists as you change direction.

little more on to your left foot at address and angle the shaft towards the target so that your hands are well in front of the ball.

In the backswing don't let your weight get any further away from the target than a 50-50 ratio. You'll need to sense a slight weight transfer from your left to your right side, but not much. The key is that you feel you're over the ball at the top of your backswing – as you can see I've clearly done at the start of this sequence. And don't forget to make a good shoulder turn.

Now for some advice straight out of the 'school of brute force'. Having made a smooth change of direction, and retained the angles in your wrists, you then have to pour on the power. Hit down hard, almost as though you're trying to hit the ball halfway up, right on its equator. Really chop it out. There's no clubhead release on this one – you want the hands to lead the club into impact and then keep the clubface as square as possible for as long as possible. It helps if you try to make sure the clubhead doesn't pass your hands through the hitting zone. You're driving the clubhead through with your forearms, your left wrist staying rock solid.

If the fairways are soft, as they were when we shot this sequence at Lake Nona in Florida, you will not believe the size of the divot-mark you'll leave in the ground. That's what brute force and steep angle of attack can do. The ball won't travel quite as far as from a good lie, but if you've done the smart thing and gone up a club, you should generate enough momentum to find the putting surface. And that's a great result.

Make sure your hands lead the clubhead into impact and that you try to keep the clubface as square as possible.

THE ART OF CHIPPING

'Think for a minute about how many greens you missed in your last competitive round of golf – go on, add them up in your head. Now think about the score you'd have shot if you'd got up and down in two just 50% of the time. My guess is you'd have won the tournament, or at least come very close.'

A LOT OF PEOPLE used to think the US Open was the major I had the least chance of winning. I don't agree with that theory. When I look back on my two victories in 1994 and 1997, I feel it wasn't such a surprise. I mean, you have to have a strong all round game to power the ball out of that thick rough that the USGA love so much! And you have to be sharp around the greens – razor sharp. I've always believed that my short game was at least as strong as any other part of my game. That week in 1994 it was *the* strongest. And it wasn't too shabby in 1997 either. Although I hit more greens than any other competitor that year, I still missed one out of four. But I kept chipping close which took pressure off my putting, enabled me to regularly get up and down for par and kept the momentum of a good round going.

Chipping is where the professionals really save shots. Look at a day's golf at one of the top tour events and you'll see greenside chip-shots holed with surprising regularity. And you'd also see that chipping stone-dead is virtually normal. I tell you, that takes a whole lot of pressure off your putting stroke.

The shots I'm going to show you in this chapter – from the basic bump-and-run to the tough cut-up shot – will give you all the knowledge you need around the greens. So instead of just hoping your chips finish close, you'll start looking to hole them.

The standard chip shot

SET UP FOR SUCCESS

There's one saying that really sums up the perfect address position for a regular chip shot and that's 'ball back, hands forward and weight forward'. Let's go through each of the three elements of that sentence, one by one.

Ball back means just what it says – you position the ball back in your stance, three or four inches inside your left heel. That's going to help you make a nice, crisp downward strike – perfect for chip shots.

Hands forward is a product of placing the ball back in the stance. As you can see here, my hands are well ahead of the clubhead, the shaft of the club and my left arm forming pretty much a straight line down towards the ball. This goes against what many

Ball back, hands forward, weight forward – the elements of a good set-up.

Make a practice swing before you chip. It helps develop a feel for the weight of the shot.

club golfers feel they want to do – they want to help the ball into the air, so they instinctively place their hands behind the ball, thinking that'll help them generate height. That's the last thing you'll get – you'll scoop the ball along the ground probably. And that's pretty depressing.

Weight forward – that's the final part. Again, it's yet another measure to help you strike down on the ball, crisply – rather than any of this awful scooping at the ball. To appreciate the right feeling, settle your weight evenly on the balls of both feet, then just bump a little more weight forward over your left foot. That should feel pretty comfortable – you can strike down on the ball pretty easily from there.

That's basically it. You need to open your stance a fraction and your knees should be comfortably flexed, but really the term 'ball back, hands forward and weight forward' takes care of pretty much everything.

Just a quick word about the grip. Choke down on the grip at least two or three inches. I always think that the closer your hands are to the clubhead the more control you have over it. And grip the club lightly – really try to feel the weight of the clubhead in your fingers. All of these things will help you judge the weight of the shot. When you're this close to the flag, direction really isn't going to be much of a problem, so your ability to judge the weight determines how close the ball finishes.

HANDS-AND-ARMS, WITH A LITTLE HINGE

Now we're all set to play the shot. If you've set up correctly to the ball, it really couldn't be more straightforward. Here I'm using a 9-iron but, as I'll demonstrate over the next few pages, you can use this technique with any club from a sand-wedge to a 6-iron. That's the great thing about this technique, it gives you a whole range of high and low shots to choose from.

The swing itself is totally controlled from the top half of your body. Your shoulders initiate the swing, the arms respond, and a light grip pressure creates that all-important feeling of 'lag' as you change direction from backswing to downswing. That's the key to chip shots of all lengths. The upper body and arms control the length and tempo of your swing and a soft, sensitive grip generates that little bit of flex, or give, in your wrists. Make a few practice swings focusing on these key thoughts – the upper body rotates, the arms swing and the hands stay soft enough to let the momentum of the swing create a softness in your wrists.

Softness shouldn't be confused with sloppy – it's far more controlled than that. Equally, you don't want to feel that the wrists are stiff or that the swing is wooden in any way as it deadens the feel in your hands.

A sensitive grip-pressure creates the necessary feeling of 'lag' as you change direction.

Ensure your hands stay ahead of the clubhead at impact.

Keep your body moving and your legs still, as your hands and arms swing through.

DRILL: *Develop 'feel' in double-quick time*

I know a lot of players who have a hard time visualising chip shots, they actually can't picture in their minds the way the ball is going to fly and how it's going to roll. My advice to those who suffer from this problem is simple, but very effective.

Grab a bag of practice balls, along with every club from a sand-wedge to a 6-iron and spend an hour or two around the practice green. Using the principles I've taught you, apply them to every club and just look at the range of shots you can play. And look how quickly you can start to threaten the hole with your chip shots.

Another drill you can do to help build a better mental image of chip shots, is to stand beside a green and gently throw balls under-arm towards the hole. Vary the height

and the distance you throw them and throw some uphill, others downhill. I bet you soon find that it's easier to judge distance when you lob the ball on a relatively low flight, and much harder when you try to lob the ball high and land it by the hole-side.

As you throw balls, keep the tempo and pace of your arm swing constant. The only thing that need change is the actual length of your arm swing, a longer swing to increase the distance and a shorter arm swing to reduce the distance. The tempo of the swing remains the same. Then from the same spot by the side of the green, grab one of your chipping clubs and try to transfer those feelings into your swing. Picture the flight of the ball on its way to the hole and the amount of run on landing. Recreate the same tempo in your swing, varying the length of your arm swings to send the ball various distances. Make a note of the height and roll characteristics every time you play a shot. Just as when you're throwing a ball underarm, I'm sure you'll find it easier to judge distance when you keep the ball low to the ground. It's really tough to judge a shot, or a throw, when you try to fly the ball all the way to the hole. I believe that if you picture chip shots as you would an under-arm throw, you'll have a better understanding of height and roll. And that can only be good for your performance.

There's no magic formula to improving your feel for chip shots. Just spend an hour a week practising your chipping and you'll be amazed at the results.

Master the method – vary the clubs

PLAYING A HIGH-FLIER

As I've already said, the great thing about the basic chip shot is that it is so easy to play. And once you know the fundamental chipping technique, you can use it to deadly effect in almost any kind of situation. How? Simply by using different degrees of loft. So having demonstrated the basic technique for you, I've really given you a whole range of shots to use around the greens.

For instance, if I take my most-lofted sand wedge I can produce a high-flying, soft-landing stroke. The swing is longer than before, but nothing much has changed really. I've got a nice, open stance and the clubface is also open to ensure the clubhead doesn't dig into the turf behind the ball. Instead, it slides nicely under the ball, lofting it quite softly towards the pin. There wouldn't be much run on this one, I can assure you.

I wouldn't normally hit a shot like this as there are no hazards between me and the flag – remember, it's easier to judge distance if you keep the ball low to the ground – but it does show what you can do with the one chipping technique.

I wouldn't normally want to play a high-flier shot from here, however...

choosing my most-lofted sand wedge demonstrates the effects of creative club selection.

PLAYING A LOW-RUNNING SHOT

Look what happens when I switch to a 6-iron. Everything stays exactly the same as it would if I was playing a sand-wedge. The ball is back in my stance, the hands are forward and my weight is forward favouring my left side. The swing is obviously much shorter, but the principles remain the same. My upper body rotates back and through, albeit only very slightly for a shot of this length, the arms swing and there's just a hint of softness and flexibility in the wrists helping to create that all important crisp, slightly downward strike. You sort of 'pop it' towards the flag.

The result couldn't be more economical. The ball just bumps forward, barely leaving the ground, before it rolls smoothly towards the hole. This is a great shot to play when there is nothing between you and the flag, maybe just a small amount of closely mown fringe grass. That's a useful rule of thumb to bear in mind when you're thinking of choosing the right shot around the green. Always land the ball on the green – whenever possible, anyway. And keep the ball as low to the ground as you can. Never use more loft than you have to – turn your chip shots into a putt as quickly as you possibly can. High, floating chip shots are harder to judge and they involve a more complicated technique. As you'll soon appreciate, there's no sense playing those shots unless you really have to.

That's the standard chip shot. I told you it was simple. Now you can imagine how, with a technique like this, just a little practice could reward you with serious results.

THE PERCENTAGE CHIPPING GAME

Here's another exercise you can do to help improve your awareness of height and roll – the two key ingredients for any chip shot. Grab a couple-of-dozen balls, ideally the same make and compression to ensure a similar feel, and divide them into three batches. Then find a green where the pin is cut roughly 10 yards from the edge. Place one batch of balls no more than a couple of paces from the green, the second batch another four or five paces away and the third batch of balls furthest away of all, say, 15 yards from the edge of the putting surface.

Starting with the shot closest to the green, use a 7-iron to chip balls at the flag. Moving back, use a 9-iron to hit the second batch of balls. Finally, switch to your sand-wedge and chip the final batch. For each shot I want you to use the standard chipping technique that I've just demonstrated. Keep the tempo of your swing the same every time, simply varying the length of your backswing to gauge distance.

Ideally, the 7-iron should cover the distance roughly 25% in the air and 75% along the ground. The 9-iron will be more like 50-50, whereas the sand-wedge will travel 75% of the distance through the air and just 25% on the ground. Repeat this drill as often as possible and don't be afraid to introduce different variables – maybe play from different types of lie and experiment with different clubs. Your feel will start to improve almost immediately and, just as importantly, you'll learn to see shots in your mind's eye which will certainly help you play the right shot, with the right club, at the right time when you're on the course.

Played with a medium iron, a low-running shot involves only a short swing.

With good ball position, you can let the loft of the club do the work for you.

This keeps the ball low to the ground and gets it rolling sooner.

The floating chip shot

Sometimes, the basic chip shot just isn't enough to get you out of trouble. You need to conjure up something a little bit special. Here's a good example. There's a bank between me and the flag – no chance of a run-up shot, then. And there isn't a great deal of room between the front edge of the green and the pin, either.

It doesn't look good, does it? Maybe this is the kind of shot you dread, especially if it's a bunker rather than a bank in front of you. If that's how you feel, I can imagine the kind of thoughts that go through your head in a competition. If that happens you're really in trouble because once you're in a negative frame of mind, it's odds-on that your next shot is from the sand.

From this position there's only one option – you've got to lob it up high in the air. The cut-up shot, one where the ball travels almost straight up in the air and lands softly, with very little run.

The first thing to tell you is that you really only want to attempt this shot from a grassy lie. Rough is no problem – there's at least plenty of grass around the ball to slide the clubhead through – but anything like a bare lie is a signal for you to look for an alternative. You may have to play to the side of the bunker, or to the fattest part of the green. That's just smart course management.

For now, though, let's assume we've got a pretty decent lie. The most obvious feature of this shot is the height, so straight away that should tell you that you need to open the clubface – and I mean really open it. Open your stance a fraction, as you would for the

A grassy lie provides the ideal setting for a cut-up shot as it allows the clubhead to slide through the grass and around the ball.

regular chip shot, and keep your weight on the left side. As for ball position, I put it a little further forward in my stance than I would for a standard chip shot. My hands are now over the ball, as opposed to ahead of it, giving me maximum loft on the clubface.

Now you basically want to try to imagine that you're swinging the club back along the line of your feet – and down along the line of your feet, too. The swing needs to be longer, so there's going to be a little bit more hingeing of the wrists in the backswing. Again, your body is the 'hub' of the swing – everything else revolves around that. I know this looks like a long swing for such a long shot, but practise will give you the nerve to swing the club back this far.

You'll need some nerve in the downswing, too. And this is where most amateurs blow their chances of hitting a good shot – they rush into the downswing, lunging at the ball, losing their height, decelerating, all kinds of things that give you no chance of success. The key here is to accelerate the clubhead smoothly through impact. Don't rush it and don't get sloppy. Just commit yourself to swinging the clubhead through the grass under the ball. Try to feel that you're almost sliding the clubhead under the ball.

And keep the clubhead swinging through impact. Don't quit on the shot – it's better to be overly positive than too tentative. And don't try to scoop the ball into the air. Let the loft of the club do the work for you – that's the easy way, believe me. Once you get the hang of this technique, the ball should pop up quite quickly and land pretty softly. Judging the distance is just a matter of feel. If you practise this shot often enough, you'll have the confidence and the 'touch' to execute it successfully when you need it most.

Hit the spot

For every chip shot you hit you have to choose a landing area and, if at all possible, it should always be on the putting surface. That way you can at least guarantee a pretty even first bounce, therefore making it easier to judge what's going to happen after that.

So when you're preparing to hit a chip shot, take a moment to stand to the side and visualise the flight of the ball. Try to imagine where the ball should land and picture the amount of roll on the ball. Then simply choose the club that you feel best performs that function. This is where practice comes in, knowing how much height and roll each club produces.

Always keep the technique nice and simple. You'll find that the standard chip shot is good enough for most situations, providing you're smart with your club selection. As I say, this entire process revolves around picking a spot on the green where you want to land the ball – and successfully hitting that spot. You can do no more than that – the rest takes care of itself.

Visualise the flight of the ball and the spot where you want it to land.

Be sure you know what height and roll each club produces and keep your technique simple.

THROW OUT A LONG-IRON AND ADD A WEDGE

Before we move on, just a quick word of advice about your equipment. You all know you're allowed to carry 14 clubs, but I'm amazed at how many club golfers don't carry their full allowance. Worse still, the number who only have one sand-wedge.

You should have three pitching clubs in your bag, minimum. In fact, a lot of professionals carry four. You should have the pitching-wedge from your standard set and at least two other wedges. One might be the sand-wedge from your set of 9 irons, with roughly 56-degrees of loft and plenty of bounce for maximum effectiveness out of bunkers. The other should be an extra-lofted utility wedge, somewhere around the 60-degrees loft mark. That's bound to be particularly useful if your home course has lots of tiny greens. With three pitching clubs in your bag, you'll have all the versatility that you need.

The parachute lob

This is a great shot to have up your sleeve. It's risky, which is why you don't see it played very often, but when you need to make the ball drop out of the sky like a stone and stop dead there's nothing quite like it. Two things to say before we get on to technique. First of all you need at least a half-decent lie, ideally a perfect one. Secondly, a 60 degree sand-wedge is the ideal club for the parachute lob. Your normal sand-wedge is OK, but it's not quite as effective at getting the job done.

The key with this shot is to deliver the maximum amount of loft possible at impact, so as to generate maximum height, so lay the clubface way open at address. You almost want it facing straight up at the sky. Position the ball opposite your left heel and open your stance, sensing that your weight is evenly spread, not favouring the left side as with most chip shots. Finally, before you swing, check that your hands are over the ball. That's unusual for a chip shot, but it's essential with the parachute lob because you don't want to hit down on the ball too steeply.

Check that the ball is opposite your left heel and your hands are over the ball.

Now we're ready to go. Swing the club back, initially along the line of your toes, into an almost three-quarter-length backswing. That part takes some getting used to when you're only looking to hit the ball, say, 20 yards. Try to keep your weight evenly spread and your legs solid – this shot doesn't call for too much movement from the hips down.

You have to generate lots of speed in the downswing, so be bold and really accelerate the clubhead through impact. As you practise this shot, try to sense that you release the clubhead a little earlier, almost as though you want the clubhead to overtake your hands through impact. You need a sweeping, not descending, angle of attack here, so make sure your weight doesn't ever get on to your left side. Get this bit right and the ball will shoot virtually straight up in the air, travelling further upwards than it does forwards. Don't anticipate much run on the ball when it sets off on a trajectory like that, so you really need to think about pitching this one on top of the flag-stick.

I really urge you to give this shot a try. As I say, it is quite tough, but there are occasions in golf when the reward justifies the risk. And besides, you can always give it a go in a fun game. Then you've got nothing to lose.

Keep your weight evenly spread as you accelerate the clubhead through the ball.

PUTTING MASTERCLASS

'Most golfers are bad putters through no fault other than their own. Think about it, no one is born a bad putter. Bad putting stems from lack of practice. When you miss that three- or four-footer, you're paying the price for neglecting the most important part of the game — getting the ball in the hole.'

HOW GOOD A PUTTER do you think you are? Well, whatever your answer to that question, the chances are you're not as good as you'd like to be. That's natural — everyone wants to hole more putts. Think back to your last competition. What would you have shot if you had taken only 27 putts? My guess is you'd have knocked at least a handful of shots off your score. Think about that — it's a huge improvement. You might have won the competition, at the very least you'd have probably beaten your handicap.

In this chapter I'm going to explain to you a few principles that will make you a better putter immediately. They're simple things. You just have to introduce them into your technique and I guarantee you will start striking the ball more consistently and on a better line. And that's going to improve your average putts per round overnight.

Then I'm going to demonstrate some drills and exercises that will really improve, and groove, your putting stroke. As I mentioned earlier, we're talking about knocking four, five, six, maybe more, off the number of putts you usually take in a round of golf. And it won't be a one-off, either. You'll be a better putter for good.

Putting — five fundamentals

THERE ARE OBVIOUSLY as many putting methods as there are people playing the game. No two are ever exactly the same. Even so, I reckon it's possible to break down the elements of any successful putting stroke into five key areas and they each relate to one another. Let's take a look at them one by one.

❶ The grip

I'm about to give a lot of attention to the grip and I make no apologies because it is more important than amateur golfers realise. Remember, your hands are the only contact with the club. It's not the sort of thing you can afford to get wrong — even in a stroke as short as a putt.

The best way to position your hands on the grip is in a neutral fashion — just as it is in the full swing. You have to try and make sure the palms are facing one another, ideally with the thumbs pointing down the centre of the shaft.

My grip is fairly orthodox. I adopt what's known as the reverse overlap grip, where my left forefinger drapes along the knuckles of my right hand. The palms are facing and the thumbs are pointing down the centre of the shaft. The only slightly unorthodox part about my grip — and it's not really that drastic — is the high left wrist position. I like this because it gives me a feeling of locking that wrist in place and therefore keeping the putter-face square to the path of my stroke, back and through.

If you're unsure about how best to grip the putter, this is the method I suggest you try. It offers the best possible chance for you to develop a putting stroke you can trust, one that can stand up to those nervy three- and four-footers you always seem to get towards the end of an important round.

Your hands work together most effectively when the palms are facing. Briefly holding your hands like this before making your proper grip will help you become more comfortable with the principle.

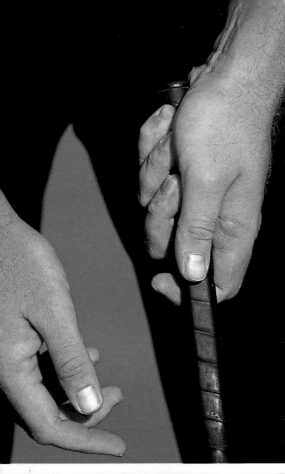

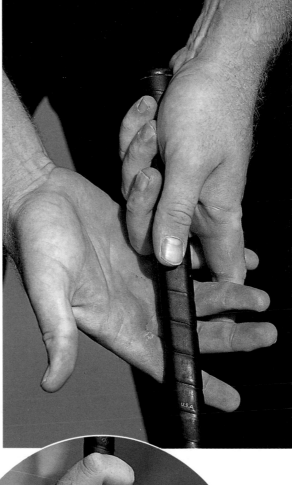

Imagine that the back of your left hand corresponds with the putter-face, square to the target, as you place it on the grip. Your thumb should point down the centre of the shaft. Entwine your right hand around your left, making sure the palms are facing one another. This is the essence of a good grip, making sure neither hand works independently.

② Your posture

How you stand to the ball on the greens is just as important as how you stand to the ball on the tee. You have to be comfortable – that's the first thing. You'll never be a good putter if you don't feel right over the ball. So relax – it can't do you any harm.

Other than that, the most important factor to keep in mind is that you have to bend from the waist in such a way that your hands and arms are free to hang down in a relaxed, comfortable fashion. This promotes a free-swinging putting stroke. And believe me, freedom of movement is essential with putting just as it is in the full swing.

Perform this quick set-up drill to check your posture. Stand upright, then bend from the waist and 'sit' a little, flexing your knees just a touch. Now let your arms hang and rest your hands very softly on your thighs. Then simply move them away from your thighs, grip the putter exactly at the point where your hands hang to. And relax. Now you're in good shape. If your arms are all hunched-up and cramped too close to your body, you can't possibly make a good stroke. I know the great Jack Nicklaus has a hunched, some might even say uncomfortable looking posture over putts, but he's not your average golfer. The fact that he can make it devastatingly effective is no reason to believe that you can do the same also.

CLUB LENGTH

Golfers often make a lot of fuss over choosing the right style of putter, but I think you need to be just as careful about the actual length of putter. The shaft must be short enough so that when you place your hands on the grip, your forearms are comfortably extended. This encourages a one-piece, pendulum putting action.

❸ Ball position

There's only one ball position that matters with putting and that's forward of centre. What I would call the 'comfort zone' – which is nicely illustrated by three balls placed between opposite my left heel and just forward of centre. Any further forward than that front ball is, in my opinion, too far forward for comfort. It throws your shoulders out of alignment – just like if you have the ball too far forward in your stance for a full shot, it drags your left shoulder left at address. I also think you're inclined to sway towards the ball, just to get at it.

If, on the other hand, you place the ball any further back than the last ball, I think you'll suffer from a tendency to hit down on your putts. And that really will cause you some problems. The ball will start jumping in the air, not rolling smoothly, and you'll never be able to judge distance consistently.

I like to see the hands over the ball in the putting stroke. You certainly don't want them behind, because that puts a kink in your left wrist, which might cause it to collapse in the stroke. Equally, I think too far forward of the ball is just as damaging. It makes you hit down on the ball – there's no chance of an upward stroke.

DRILL: *Let gravity determine ball position*

Positioning your eyes directly over the ball enables you to line up more effectively and also gives you a more accurate perspective when looking down the line of a putt. So take a minute every now and then to check for sure that your eyes are directly over the ball. It's the simplest of procedures. Get comfortable first, adopting your normal putting posture, then drop a golf ball from the bridge of your nose. Gravity takes care of the rest. Where it strikes the ground is the exact spot where you should position it in your stance.

This procedure is simplicity itself yet it helps you monitor one of the keys to better putting.

❹ Retain the triangle

In the stroke itself, I think you just need a couple of key thoughts to ensure that your putting stroke runs smoothly. Any more than that and you'll be rigid with tension. You'll also probably stand over the ball for an age as you try to put all the various moves and keys into some sort of order. Not a good thing.

So keep it simple. That's the best approach.

See the triangle here formed by my arms and shoulders. When I'm really putting well I like to think that this triangle stays intact all through the stroke.

Give it a try. As you move the putter back, your shoulders should rock, and your hands stay pretty passive. Now from there you just need to rock your shoulders back and accelerate the putter into the back of the ball. Don't go meddling with your hands or getting all 'wristy' – just keep your left wrist firm and strike the back of the ball. If your ball position is correct, you'll strike the ball ever-so-slightly on the up-stroke – just what you need to put a smooth roll on the putt.

Form the triangle at address and retain it throughout the stroke – it's as simple as that.

One final thing. You'll see in my stroke that my left elbow and wrist stay high all the way through impact. I like the way that feels, to me it kind of helps stop my left wrist breaking down. You don't have to do that, but it is important that the left wrist stays firm as you accelerate the putter-head through the ball. If your left wrist 'breaks down' you will miss the putt, guaranteed.

DRILL: *Rock the shaft for a perfect pendulum stroke*

I think any stroke that relies heavily on the hands and wrists is inclined to be a little unpredictable, particularly if the 'heat' gets turned up a bit. Under pressure, and any other time, a shoulder-controlled, pendulum-type stroke is going to produce more consistent results. And that's the name of the game.

Try the following practice drill to help enhance the sensations of a shoulder-dominated, pendulum putting stroke. Adopt a good, comfortable posture and then trap the shaft of a club under your armpits so that its nice and snug across your chest *(see below)*. As you look down you'll see a triangle formed by the shaft of the club and your forearms and hands. What you need to do is feel that you rock that triangle back and forth as you hit balls. Concentrate on keeping that 'unit' working together, your hands maintaining a soft hold on the club so that the putter-head flows back and through with a syrupy-smooth

rhythm. Mentally, I want you to feel that the ball isn't there. Just concentrate on your stroke and let the ball merely get in the way of the swinging putter-head.

Within a few minutes of starting this drill, you'll start to feel that everything works in unison, the entire movement controlled by the rocking motion of your shoulders. There's no need for your hands to go 'flicky' or for your wrists to buckle and bend. Just spend a few minutes working on this drill, once or twice a week, and it will certainly help you integrate a shoulder-dominated action into your proper stroke. I believe you'll see some really positive results come from that change.

⑤ Length of stroke determines distance

One of the big differences between amateurs and professionals lies in the pace of the stroke. Lots of amateurs have a tendency to maintain a similar length stroke for most putts and apply varying degrees of force in the downswing to send the ball the required distance. The professional, on the other hand, varies the length of the stroke and maintains the same tempo, whatever the range. A far more reliable system.

I want you to start thinking more like the professionals. Try to maintain the same pace and tempo in your putting stroke, varying the distance you hit the ball by varying the length of your stroke. One final thing: with every putt you hit – from long rakers to tap-in tiddlers; from slick downhillers to steep uphillers – you have to accelerate the putter into the back of the ball. I don't care how slick the greens are, you have to go through faster than you went back. That's a rule you can't afford to break.

With short putts like this, economy of movement is essential. You simply can't afford too many moving parts. Just keep your stroke tidy going back and accelerate the putter into the ball.

Now, as you move further away from the hole, you need to work on the principle of gradually increasing the length of your stroke accordingly. The actual tempo remains unchanged.

Pressure putting — you need a routine

Pressure is a funny thing. Some golfers on a great score will fall apart towards the end of the round. Most will privately confess to getting a little defensive. Others, admittedly a very small minority, continue to play their own game. These are the golfers that make great champions — the greater the occasion, the better they play. There are many ways we can learn from such golfers.

I think one of the keys to holing out under pressure is to learn to treat even the important putts just like any other putt. To do that you have to develop a routine. A routine you can trust and, most crucially of all, a routine you can repeat.

Whenever I'm faced with a vital putt, I go through the same procedure I've gone through for years. Whether I'm on the 1st green of a regular tour event or the 72nd green of a major championship, I try to treat every putt the same.

1 *To start with, I place the ball in such a way that the maker's name lines up with the line along which I want the ball to start rolling.*

2 *Next, I'll take a look from behind the ball — that's my 'main read'.*

3 *Whichever is the low side, that's where I'll wander down to in order to get a different perspective on the putt.*

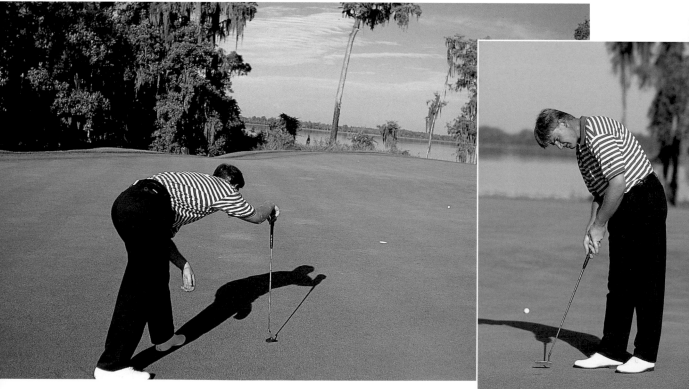

4 *Next, a brief look from behind the hole to confirm my line. I might even rehearse a little practice putting stroke near the hole, if that's where I visualise the ball breaking from.*

5 *Then it's back behind the ball to gather my thoughts and two slow, smooth practice strokes. As I'm doing this, I try to flood my mind with positive images about the perfect speed and line. I try to actually visualise the ball rolling towards the hole.*

6Once I'm over the ball I take two looks at the hole, then I pull the trigger. That's it.

That sounds like a long routine, but it really isn't that time consuming. Besides, you probably won't want to go through quite so many stages. For one thing, if you play most of your golf on the one course, which I obviously don't, then you'll know the breaks and borrows on each of the 18 greens. That eliminates the need to read greens in the amount of detail I've just demonstrated.

I do urge you though, next time you play try to be aware of the way you prepare to putt. How many, if any, practice strokes do you take? How many times do you look at the hole as you address the ball? Make a mental note of all these things and try to repeat the exact same routine on the next green, and the green after that. As I've said, a routine needn't be a recipe for slow play. Go about it in a brisk fashion and try to keep your wits about you when your partners are putting — you can save a lot of time by preparing to putt long before it's actually your turn.

Eventually your routine will become almost second nature. And when you come to the 18th green in a competition, tell yourself it's just another putt. Just another routine job to do. If you can repeat your normal routine, right down to the number of practice strokes you take and the number of times you look at the hole, you stand a far better chance of making a good stroke. And you can't ask any more of yourself than that.

The art of reading greens

Reading greens is a funny business. Most people know which way the ball breaks on the greens at their home course, but away from home it's an altogether different story. Some golfers just happen to be better than others, but it's tough to put your finger on exactly why they are good in this particular department. Well, I consider myself a pretty good reader of greens, so all I can do in this section is pass on a few of the things I look for in a putt, the tell-tale signs indicating which way the ball will break.

1   *Take a good look at the whole green as you approach it. I often find that from a distance I can get a pretty good idea of the lie of the land and that's my first clue as to what breaks the ball might take.*

2   *Look from behind the ball and look from the side. It needn't take an age – if you're smart you can usually find time in-between your playing partners hitting their approach chips or putts.*

3   *Look at what your playing partner's ball does as it approaches the hole. Even if he's not coming from exactly the same line as you, you can still learn a lot about how the ball behaves in that crucial last 18 inches or so of its journey to the hole.*

4   *Remember, speed determines break. A firmly struck putt breaks less than a ball hit at a slower speed. So, decide how firmly you want to hit the putt, then establish how much the ball will move at that speed.*

5   *Some golfers find it hard to believe that wind can affect the line of a putt, but it does. Obviously a light breeze isn't going to do anything, but if your trouser bottoms are flapping, then that should alert you to the fact that it is strong enough to make a difference. And the faster the greens, the more the wind will influence the ball's path to the hole. It can cancel out the break on some putts, or increase the swing on others.*

6   *Finally, experiment a little. I can't show you the break on putts, so the best thing you can do is work on a trial and error basis. During the next practice round you play, some balls around a hole – say, 15 feet away – and try to read each putt individually. Then hit the putt and see if you were right. If you read it incorrectly, take a second look and see if you can see the line now. Bit by bit, you're training your eyes to see the borrows and spot the tell-tale signs. And that really is what reading greens is all about. You can't just suddenly become a good line-reader overnight. Like anything else, it takes experience.*

If you don't think you're very good at reading greens, set up some balls aound the hole as shown here. Read each putt individually, slowly working your way around the circle.

TIP: *Putt to a breaking point...*

I see a lot of golfers get themselves in a real tangle on breaking putts, particularly those where there's a lot of swing involved. First, they have an alignment problem at address and then they tend to want to guide the ball, which results in a crooked stroke. That's the recipe for a lot of badly struck, and badly missed, putts.

There's an easy and reliable solution to this, though, and it's a system I have used myself. What it involves is putting to a 'breaking point'. Assess the line of a putt and identify a spot where you feel the ball will start turning towards the hole – in a practice situation you can use a tee-peg as I have here. Then treat that spot as an intermediate target – don't forget about the hole, but for now just focus on that spot. Align yourself and the putter-face accordingly and then go ahead and putt towards that spot. Obviously you need to factor-in the right speed, but other than that it's just a case of stroking the ball towards your breaking point and simply letting the natural contour of the green take care of the rest. Simple.

Use a tee-peg to indicate the break, set the ball off at that mark and let gravity do the rest.

TIP: ...*or treat every putt as a straight putt*

Another method you can adopt on breaking putts, one that I know is favoured by a lot of good players, is to treat every putt as a straight putt. The principle is similar to the 'breaking point' system, but not identical. There's one important difference. Say you've read a putt and seen a 12-inch break from the right. Well, what you do is visualise an imaginary hole 12 inches right of the real hole. That's your target. The actual hole may as well not exist – you have to putt to the imaginary hole. Again, in a practice situation you can use a prop, such as a golf ball as I have here, to indicate your imaginary hole.

What you're basically doing is treating every putt as a straight putt, which as I'm sure you'll appreciate is bound to help you make a better, more on-line stroke. You won't feel the need to guide the ball, or anything like that. And, just as is the case with the 'breaking point' system, once you've committed yourself to the line, you can simply allow the slope of the green to do the work for you. I like the idea of this method – anything that simplifies slope putting has to be a good thing.

This is a useful practice drill to help eliminate doubt on breaking putts.

Different strokes work for different folks

Putting is open to greater personal interpretation than any other aspect of the game, which is why you see some weird and wonderful styles, not just at club level but on the pro circuits, too. If you find things aren't working in your stroke, you might like to try the cross-handed method.

This really is quite popular now in the professional ranks. While this method isn't for me, I can see the advantages. For one thing it keeps your shoulders more level at address, instead of the right shoulder being lower than the left as would normally be the case. This helps produce a lower-to-the-ground takeaway and a smooth, on-the-up stroke into impact. So the ball rolls pretty well.

It also means the right hand is less dominant and the left wrist stays pretty much locked in place through the hitting area. A firm left wrist is crucial in any successful stroke because it encourages the putter-face to stay square throughout, which obviously translates into more on-line putts. Be prepared to give it time, though, and make an effort to get used to it.

The crosss-handed putting stroke helps keep the left wrist firm throughout, thus ensuring the putter-face stays square at impact.

TIP: MAKER'S NAME SHOWS YOU THE LINE TO THE HOLE

Virtually every tour player I know places the ball a certain way when they prepare to putt. Mostly it's out of habit, sometimes superstition. But one thing's for sure, for most professionals there's nothing random about marking and replacing the ball on the green.

What a lot of amateurs don't realise is that there are actually some benefits to placing the ball a certain way. The most common method is having the maker's name aligned so that it runs along the target line – kind of showing you the line to the hole I guess. As I've already explained, this is the method I choose. It may seem insignificant, but as a visual aid it can really help focus your mind on rolling the ball, end over end, down the intended line. If it helps create those positive mental pictures, even in the tiniest way, then it's well worth doing.

Another method is to have the maker's name on the back portion of the ball, exactly where the putter-face makes contact. This helps you concentrate on accelerating the putter into something specific which, say, when you're a long way from the hole, encourages you to be positive. I know for a fact that Gary Player has favoured this method from time to time over the years.

Little things like this can often 'click' you into positive frame of mind. In a way it's all part of the routine I referred to earlier in this chapter, a routine which can make such a huge difference to your performances on the greens.

Two types of fringe — two types of stroke

PUTT FROM THE FIRST CUT...

Here's a situation that happens a lot on courses with fast, sloping greens and probably several times at your home club, too. The ball has just come to rest against the cut of the fringe that forms the edge of the green, making the ball difficult to get at in an orthodox way. Time for a touch of improvisation, then.

Take your putter and hover the clubhead above the surface of the fringe grass, literally in mid-air. You might want to grip down on the putter an inch now that the putter-head is an inch above the ground, just so your set-up feels more natural.

Hover the putter-head above the fringe grass and make your regular stroke.

From an address position like this, you're going to automatically hit the ball just above its equator just by making your regular, every-day putting stroke. This is essentially what you want, because it imparts lots of top-spin and thus puts a nice smooth roll on the putt. However, this does mean that you have to concentrate doubly-hard on staying down throughout the stroke. Any lifting up, or peeking too soon, will cause you to top the ball completely. And if that happens, apart from being totally embarrassing, it's unlikely the ball will make it even halfway to the hole. Also, don't try to hit down into impact because the ball will jump severely off the putter-face making it very difficult to judge speed.

Providing you keep your head still and trust your stroke, you'll put a nice smooth roll on the ball.

...AND FLIP A SAND-WEDGE FROM THE SECOND CUT

If that last shot needs a touch of improvisation, this shot needs a ton of the stuff. The scenario is pretty identical, only this time the ball has come to rest between the fringe grass and the first cut of rough. With the grass standing so much taller behind the ball, it makes life very tricky indeed.

   This in my opinion is no job for the putter. I know some professionals toe-poke this one with the putter, but that strikes me as being awfully risky. Besides, it's impossible with the way many putters are designed these days.

   Here's a better method by far. Grab a sand-wedge and adopt your normal putting grip and stance, hovering the clubhead as near to the level of the ball as the fringe grass will allow. Feel as though your hands and arms are simply hanging down, almost limp.

Assume your normal putting stance and literally hinge your wrists to get some backswing.

Then, keeping your wrists super-soft and pliable, flip the club back and forth almost letting the weight of the clubhead do the work for you. You don't really need to apply any force of your own and the arms barely move. As I say, you just need to hinge your wrists softly back and through, hitting the ball bang-square on its equator, definitely no higher-up than that.

It's a technique that will feel quite strange at first, but give it a try in practice and I think you'll be surprised at the quality and consistency of the results you can achieve. It's only good for shots up to about 20 feet but it is a very imaginative and effective way out of a tough little spot close to the flag. These pictures don't show it, but this one actually lipped out... first attempt. There is no reason why you can't do the same.

'Flip' the clubhead into the back of the ball. Your arms barely move position from set-up.

Perfect practice makes for a perfect putting stroke

I HAVEN'T MET A SINGLE amateur who enjoyed practising their putting. Not one. Having seen the way they practise before pro ams, though, it's not surprising. To me it doesn't look like they know what they want to achieve or what they want to work on. There's no purpose to it. I mean, just knocking a few balls about with no real pattern seems pretty aimless.

If you just stand on the putting green and tap balls about, without really thinking much about what you're doing, I can't see what use that is to you. You almost may as well not do it at all. Whenever you practise your putting, or any other part of your game for that matter, you've got to have some idea of why you are there and what you are trying to achieve. In this section, then, I will be demonstrating a selection of tried-and-tested drills and exercises that are designed to make you a better putter and a more consistent one. Many are used by professionals out on tour and my guess is that they will help you enjoy practising your putting a lot more. So it's good news all round.

DRILL: *Putt 'blind' for ultra-sensitive feel*

They say that if you take away one of your five senses, then the remaining four have to work overtime in order to compensate. Well, this exercise is based on that theory.

Start with eight or nine balls down by your side. Address the first one, then close your eyes and putt. It doesn't really matter how far you stroke the first ball, just so long as it isn't a few feet in front of you, or so far away as to be ridiculous. I guess roughly 10-15 feet is about right. Then one-by-one work your way through the remaining balls, each time closing your eyes just prior to starting the stroke. Concentrate on staying relaxed and maintaining a nice smooth tempo. Just let the ball get in the way of the swinging putter-head. Ideally, you want to get to the stage where the balls end up quite closely grouped together – inside a two-foot radius, from this sort of range, would be a very good result.

I suggest you try this exercise first without a hole. It has several benefits. For one thing, not having to worry about a hole will introduce more freedom into your stroke immediately, because you're not so direction-conscious. Also, you start to think more in terms of the actual feel of your stroke, rather than being overly mechanical, because it's all you've got to go on. And that's a major plus-point, too.

As you grow in confidence, putt towards a hole as I have here. You'll get quite a pleasant surprise when you find yourself holing putts with your eyes closed. And just think how much more confident you'll be with them open!

Close your eyes, stay relaxed...

and maintain a nice smooth tempo.

DRILL: *Putt around the compass points*

Putting from around the hole isn't a new idea, but I reckon it's still the best exercise there is for improving your holing-out ratios. It's up to you how few or how many balls you use, but I would say three in each row is more than enough. The important thing is to tailor the exercise to suit your own standards. If you're a bit shaky on the short putts, don't go setting the first 'set' of balls four feet away from the hole. You'll miss more than you hole and what does that do? Leave your confidence in tatters, that's what. So build up gradually. Start from 12 inches away and get used to banging the ball into the back of the hole. Enjoy it, get your confidence on a high.

Then move back gradually. Set yourself some two footers. Then when you're holing those, regular as clockwork, move back again this time to three feet – you should still be able to knock in most of those without too much bother. As an alternative for this exercise, try using four balls only and place them around the hole at 12 o'clock, 3 o'clock, 6 o'clock and 9 o'clock. Ideally, you want a hole that is cut on a slope, so you have one uphill putt, one downhill, one left-to-right and one right-to-left. Move around the clockface, holing out from each hour. Just as with the previous exercise, start from close range so that you can build up your confidence gradually. It's always best to start easy and build up slowly.

There are many variations to this exercise. Just be sure not to start too far away.

DRILL: *Establish face alignment*

If you're missing a lot of shortish putts, the probable cause could be one of two things. Either the alignment of the putter-face is crooked or the path of your stroke through impact is off-line. Oh, there is a third option, of course – they could both be wrong! Anyway, whatever the case you need to put it right pretty quickly or else you're in for some miserable rounds of golf. This straightforward exercise can do that for you.

First, find yourself a dead-straight four-foot putt. Now address it as you would normally. Give a thought to your grip pressure and be sure that it is light. Tensing up will not do you any good. Now, instead of making a normal stroke, simply brush the ball towards the hole *(see above)*. Don't make a backswing, not even the slightest hint of one. Basically, just make a followthrough. What this does is train you to get the putter-face square at address and then travelling on a straight-line path towards the hole. They are the two key ingredients for holing those 'shorties'. If any of your attempts miss, then as I said earlier either the path of your stroke or the putter-face alignment is wrong. Try again. You'll get it right eventually and when you do, you'll know that you're 'brushing' on the right lines.

One thing you might want to do is have a friend stand behind you and provide confirmation that the putter-face is aligned correctly to begin with. This could eliminate one of the mistakes right from the outset.

DRILL: *Putt along the shaft to control path*

If your putting stroke doesn't have good path, then you'll never be able to control the direction of your putts. And that's not a good way to go about getting the ball in the hole. These few exercises that I'm demonstrating here are designed to help you on two counts. First, you'll begin to understand what the correct path for the putter should be. And second, it will help you groove that correct path on a consistent basis, thus creating the necessary muscle memory to repeat a good stroke on the golf course.

Find a dead-straight six-foot putt and lay a club on the ground, just inside the ball and parallel to the ball-to-hole line, as I have here *(see below)*. Try to establish an address position that sets your eye-line, your shoulders and your hips parallel to that shaft. Your feet can be a little open if you like. Now, having checked to make sure that the putter-face is also square, run the putter straight back and through along a path parallel to the shaft.

Simply let the ball get in the way of a good stroke. That's all you have to do.

Have a dozen or so balls handy, so that you can repeat the exercise without a break. From this distance, the perfect path is straight back and straight through – only when you move further away does the putter-head start to travel inside the line in the backswing. And even then it still should travel straight along the line of the putt in the followthrough – that bit never changes.

An alternative exercise *(see right)* is to run the putter over the top of the shaft, making repeated practice strokes. Again, try to set your eye-line level with the shaft on the ground. That way you can swivel your head to the left and be looking straight down the target line. You don't have to alter your head position in any way to get a good mental picture of the ball's path to the hole. And remember, for any putt inside, say, eight feet make sure the putter stays on a dead-straight path back and through. Once you're happy with your practice stroke 'over the rails', step back, address the ball for real and repeat it, simply letting the ball get in the way.

These are exercises I've rehearsed probably hundreds of times in hotel rooms around the world. As well as filling-in some of the inevitable lonely times on tour, it's had a great effect on my putting stroke over the years. Try to find a little bit of time to do the same exercises at home. Honestly, just a few minutes here and there will make a big difference to the quality and consistency of your putting stroke. If it's good enough for me, it's good enough for you.

DRILL: *Maintaining a 'steady head'*

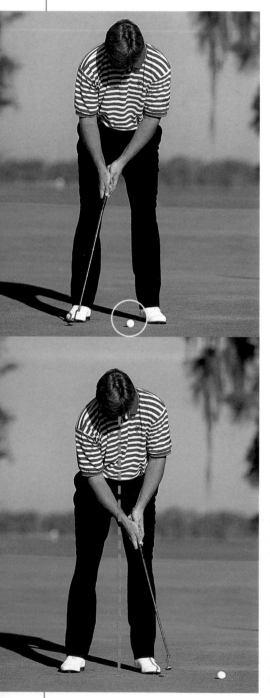

Looking up too soon in the putting stroke is something that every golfer who ever lived has done from time to time. Some are regular offenders, others do it under moments of intense pressure. Whatever the case, it usually stems from a lack of belief or confidence. Basically you're so eager for the ball to go in the hole that you can't resist having a peek. But as soon as your head moves, so do the shoulders and the arms. And that knocks your stroke off line at the single most critical moment, just as you're about to hit the ball. That early peek usually results in a disappointing view.

Here's a simple exercise to train you to stop peeking too soon. Place a tiny object under the ball or under the putter-head at address *(top)*. I'm using a pine needle here, but a coin or ball-marker is just as effective. Then as you make your stroke simply focus on that object *(bottom)*. Forget about everything else for the moment, just keep your eyes fixed on that spot. Hit a succession of putts, working solely on this one key thought. Literally in the space of a few minutes it will feel perfectly natural to keep your head down long after the ball is on its way. And then you've cracked it. All you need to do is remove the object from under the ball and transfer those same thoughts into your proper stroke. It will help you enormously on short putts, when the temptation to look up is at its greatest, but it's an equally good thought to have on long putts because it's bound to help you strike the ball more consistently out of the sweet-spot.

Once on the golf course you obviously can't use props like pine needles and ball-markers to help you. But you can achieve the same results on short putts by committing yourself to not looking up until you hear the ball drop into the hole. That'll stop you looking up too soon for sure.

DRILL: *Random targets for the ultimate test*

Here's another exercise. It's possibly the best way I know for helping improve your judgement of distance. Take five tee-pegs and stick them in the putting green at various distances and directions, so that you've got a mixture of different break putts and different length putts. Now work your way through, say 20 balls, making sure you never hit two putts in succession to the same tee-peg.

Putting to random targets in this way is great practice because it simulates an on-course situation where you've got one chance to get it right and one chance only. Tee-pegs are especially useful targets because you can move them around the green at will, thus varying the lengths of putts and also the breaks. Make sure you vary the position of the tees. In this exercise, you don't ever want to get to the stage where you're familiar with any given putt.

Place tee-pegs around the green and never putt to the same one twice in succession.

DRILL: *Stroke and distance – it's the only way*

Grab about half-a-dozen balls from your golf bag and starting at around eight feet, place the balls in a line away from the hole. Ideally, choose a green that has a fair amount of slope on it. How far apart you space the balls depends on the size of the green – if it's massive you can make the gap between balls as wide as five or six feet. On a smaller green you may have to reduce the gap down to something like three feet.

The distance you choose is irrelevant, though. What is important is that the tempo of your stroke stays the same for every single one of those putts. As you work your way back from the hole, the only thing that changes is the length of your stroke, relatively short for the first putt, increasing in length gradually as you work through the exercise. It's just like the full swing where your tempo and rhythm should feel the same from wedge up to driver. The theory for putting is exactly the same – you must maintain a consistent tempo in your stroke. It's perhaps the single biggest step towards becoming a good 'lag' putter. That means you'll hole more mid-to-long range putts and, just as importantly, three-putt far less often. And isn't that what we all want.

Start with the putt nearest the hole then gradually work your way back.

DRILL: *Warming-up before your round*

If you're warming-up before a round, then I think you have to be very careful how you practise your putting. Obviously, it's a bit too late in the day to be working on anything overly technical. So I see the main object of the exercise as trying to gain a feel for the pace and tempo of your stroke and the pace of the greens. Maybe you can also find yourself a key thought for the day to take on to the course with you, something that just feels right at the time and which helps you focus on making a good stroke.

Try to get a feel for distance – hit a few long putts and concentrate solely on making an unhurried, smoothly accelerating stroke. Hit a few short putts, by all means. But be careful. It's better to not hit any at all than miss a load before you go out.

One final thought about the putter, don't be afraid to use this club from off the green. It's a shot that golfers are often embarrassed to play, as though putting from off the green is some kind of kop-out. Well that's nonsense. There are many situations just off the green where a putter is the smart club to play. You'll see a lot of the world's best players, in any Open Championship, putt from yards and yards off the green. The fact is, when the grass is closely mown between you

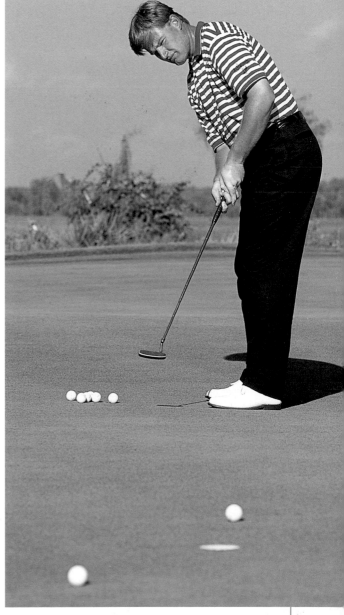

and the putting surface, I can't see anything wrong with keeping the ball on the ground. In the right place at the right time it's just as easy to judge as a chip and certainly a lot easier to play. So don't ever rule it out.

SAND PLAY MADE SIMPLE

'I know you've probably heard or read at least 100 people say bunker play is easy, but it really is. Believe me. The trouble with most club golfers is they set up to the ball incorrectly, which creates havoc with the swing, and generally have a poor grasp of the few fundamentals upon which successful sand play is built.'

IF I DID A SURVEY of club golfers asking them their least favourite shot, I reckon most would say the bunker shot. Not all, but most. Even if you don't think it's your worse shot, you still probably don't hit too many bunker shots close to the hole. You may even still leave a few in the sand — and that gets expensive.

Compare this with most professionals. They'd rather be in the sand, assuming a decent lie, than in the rough. I know I would. It's easier to control the ball from sand and the technique is no more difficult than a chip shot. You don't even have to hit the ball — you just let the sand do the work for you.

Once you understand the basic techniques and then develop a bit of confidence you will be amazed at how well you can start playing those greenside bunker shots. You'll wonder whatever the fuss was all about.

So let's get on with it.

The tools of the sand trade

THE FIRST THING I want you to understand is that your sand-wedge is designed to help you a lot more than you probably realise. Gene Sarazen, a golfer known as 'The Squire', and one of only four players to have won all four major championships, invented this club way back in the 1930s. And he did it for a good reason. The wide flange on the sole of the club encourages the clubhead to slide through the sand. And that is the essence of good bunker play. The clubhead slides through the sand, throwing the ball up and out on to the green. This is known as the 'bounce effect'. In many ways though it is better to think of it as the 'splash effect'. The clubhead splashes the ball out on a cushion of sand.

If you have a sharp leading edge, which was the case with the pre-1930s sand-wedge and every other iron club in your bag today, the clubhead tends to dig into the sand rather than slide through it. And from a decent lie that's definitely not what you want. That's why Gene Sarazen re-invented the sand-wedge. If it weren't for his good thinking, you can be certain that bunker play would be a lot more difficult today. Not a nice thought, is it?

The standard greenside bunker shot

SET-UP RULES YOU CAN'T AFFORD TO IGNORE

Bunker play becomes 10-times easier if you stick to a few basic principles at address – and 100-times more difficult if you ignore them. So before I even let you hit another bunker shot, I'm going to show you how to address the ball correctly for the regular greenside splash. Bear with me here because a little attention to detail at this early stage is going to accelerate the learning, and ultimately improving, process.

First things first. The bounce effect on your sand-wedge works best when the clubface is open – there's absolutely no way that clubface can dig too deep into the sand if it stays open. So that's your first principle of good bunker play, you have to open the clubface at address so that it actually faces right of the flag (see inset). It's important that you open the clubface first and then form your grip, which should be a little weaker than normal. If you grip it first and then open the face, it'll return to square at impact and cause you problems with height and accuracy.

Open your stance, too. That means your shoulders, hips and toes need to be aiming, say, 30 feet left of the target. Spread your weight pretty evenly on both feet and, as you look down at your grip, I want you to check that your hands are level with the ball, maybe even a fraction behind it. Finally, ease the pressure on your grip approximately 20% to ensure a nice, sensitive hold on the club. Now you're in good shape.

Swing along your body-line

The key now is to swing along the line of your toes and body – that's why the angles you establish at address are so important. Using a harmonious blend of body rotation and arm swing, try to make sure the clubhead follows the line of your toes as you swing it smoothly away from the ball. Then hinge your wrists to 'set' the club in position at the top. Keep your grip pressure light and, as you change direction into your downswing, you'll sense a little bit of 'lag' in your hands and wrists. That's good.

Now focus on an exact spot a couple of inches behind the ball to help regulate your point of entry and swing the clubhead through the sand. Your open stance will ensure that the clubhead travels on the necessary out-to-in path, but it helps if you sense that

Start the club back along the line of your toes and hinge your wrists to 'set' the club at the top.

your hands stay close to your body through impact. The design of your sand-wedge will take care of the rest for you. Also, note my knees stay nice and flexed, stabilising my swing as the club swings back and forth. The ball sets off a little left of target and then spins to the right, with a little bit of run on landing.

Once you've sorted out your technique, controlling distance will come a lot sooner than you think. Remember in the chapter on putting, I recommended that you control distance by varying the length of your stroke. The same theory works well in sand. Simply alter the distance you want the ball to fly by lengthening or shortening your swing. The actual tempo of your swing and the pace at which you accelerate the clubhead through the sand should feel pretty much the same every time. That's a far more reliable method than trying to hit harder or softer from identical length swings.

Splash the clubhead down into the sand behind the ball and always follow through.

How to make the ball fly high and sit down

When there isn't much green to work with, as you can see here where the pin is cut tight to the left side of the green, I adapt my technique slightly to produce a higher, softer trajectory with virtually no run on the ball. I also use my 60-degree, rather than my 56-degree, sand-wedge. Maximum loft for maximum height.

The changes you need to make couldn't be easier. Place the ball more central in your stance *(see inset)* and feel that your weight favours your left side just a fraction. Then in your swing consciously hinge your wrists a little earlier in the takeaway, basically pointing the shaft of the club more at the sky. That establishes the steeper swing plane that you need for this shot.

In the downswing there are two things to bear in mind. Firstly, take a little less sand at impact – aim to hit behind the ball, say, one inch instead of two. Secondly, make a slightly longer swing than you would for a regular bunker shot from the same distance and really 'zip' the clubhead through the sand under the ball to help generate the extra carry necessary to get it to the hole.

> ### TIP: CHOKE DOWN ON THE GRIP FOR MAXIMUM FEEL
>
> *With bunker shots, and 99% of all other shots around the green, I always think it's best to grip down on the club a couple of inches. By shortening the club in this way, you bring your hands closer to the ball. And for my money, that can only improve your feel for distance. If you think about it, judgement of speed is the most important part of a great short game. Being so close to the hole, accuracy is never going to be that much of a problem. At least it shouldn't be, anyway. So grip down and hone in on that flag.*

Take these thoughts into the bunker with you and commit yourself to being 100% positive. Remember, with this shot, the ball will have virtually no run on landing so you can afford to pitch it right up to the flag. Get this one right and it's a very satisfying, spectacular-looking shot.

For a high-flying bunker shot, take less sand and really 'zip' the clubhead through impact.

DRILL: *Right-handed swings keep the clubhead moving*

There are two features of good bunker play that are worth mentioning again. First is the necessity to keep the clubhead moving through the sand. This sounds obvious, but I mean keep it moving in a smooth, flowing motion. Sadly, I don't see that too often when amateurs play this shot. Second is the angle of attack. The clubhead needs to swing on a shallow path into the sand, not a steeply descending one. The following exercise gives you the right feeling for both.

Assume good bunker play posture and take your left hand off the grip. Let your left hand hang free or put it in your pocket or behind your back, whatever feels most comfortable. Also, open the clubface. Now using your right hand only, make slow, rhythmical, almost lazy practice swings down and through the sand. Grip mega-lightly and keep the movement very free, almost as though you are letting go of the club.

Notice how the clubhead just slides through the sand? You don't even have to force it. And the clubhead doesn't bury itself, either. Simply the weight of the club and the momentum of a free swing give you the two key ingredients I was talking about – a shallow angle of attack and a smoothly accelerating swing. Introduce the sensations from this practice drill into your proper swing and you've cracked it. You'll have a better technique in no time at all.

DRILL: *Draw a line in the sand for a consistent splash*

Being able to hit the same spot in the sand behind the ball is one of the principal keys to consistent bunker play because it enables you to predict exactly how the ball will come out of the sand, therefore making it easier to judge distance. When you're practising your bunker play, try drawing a line in the sand roughly one ball's-width behind the ball. Then concentrate on slicing the clubhead into the sand on that exact spot and swinging through to a finish. Once you start to hit that spot consistently, you can then start to experiment with different length shots. Keep hitting the same spot in the sand and simply vary the length of your swing to control the distance the ball flies through the air.

As well as fine-tuning your technique to a high degree, this exercise really will bring your 'mental game' to a new level. The thought of leaving the ball in the sand won't even enter

your head. Instead, you'll be picturing the flight of the shot and thinking about where you want the ball to land on the green.

You can even carry this theory on to the golf course to help you hit better bunker shots. Obviously you can't draw lines with your finger, but you can focus on a precise spot in the sand rather than looking at the ball itself. So do just that. Concentrate on a spot a couple of inches behind the ball and just go ahead and hit it. You don't even have to worry about the ball, because as long as you hit your spot and follow through, it will come out every time.

One final thing. From a decent lie, the ideal 'divot mark' in the sand should be long and shallow, roughly the size of a bank note. If the divot you leave in the sand is much bigger, I would say you're taking too much sand. Any smaller and you're not taking enough sand.

Upslope lies

BE MORE AGGRESSIVE

A bunker shot from an upslope lie is considerably easier than a shot from a downhill lie, which is why we're looking at this one first. The beauty of an uphill lie is that it gives you licence to be so much more aggressive. You can make a really positive swing and fly the ball right up to the hole, knowing almost for certain that it's going to stick to the green like a dart in a board.

Your set-up is again critically important. The basic rule for any shot from a sloping lie states that you have to settle your weight on your lower leg. That's your starting point, so sense that most of your weight is supported over your right knee. What this does is bring your shoulders into a more neutral position relative to the slope. They're basically more level. Other than that, you need to concentrate on keeping your stance and the clubface a little squarer than you would for a regular bunker shot. Also, position the ball a couple of inches more forward than normal – roughly opposite your left heel.

Keep your weight pretty steady as you swing – there's no swaying allowed here on this shot. In the downswing (see over the page), swing with the slope and be aggresive. The one potential danger in playing from an upslope is that it's easy to leave the ball short, so you have to hit the sand as close to the ball as possible without thinning it. That should help you generate extra momentum at impact — and therefore greater distance. As an extra measure to guard against leaving the ball well short, try to imagine you want the ball to hit the flag-stick halfway up. That should encourage you to be more aggressive, thus giving your swing the extra 'zip' that you'll need for an upslope lie.

Settle your weight over your right knee for
maximum stability in your swing.

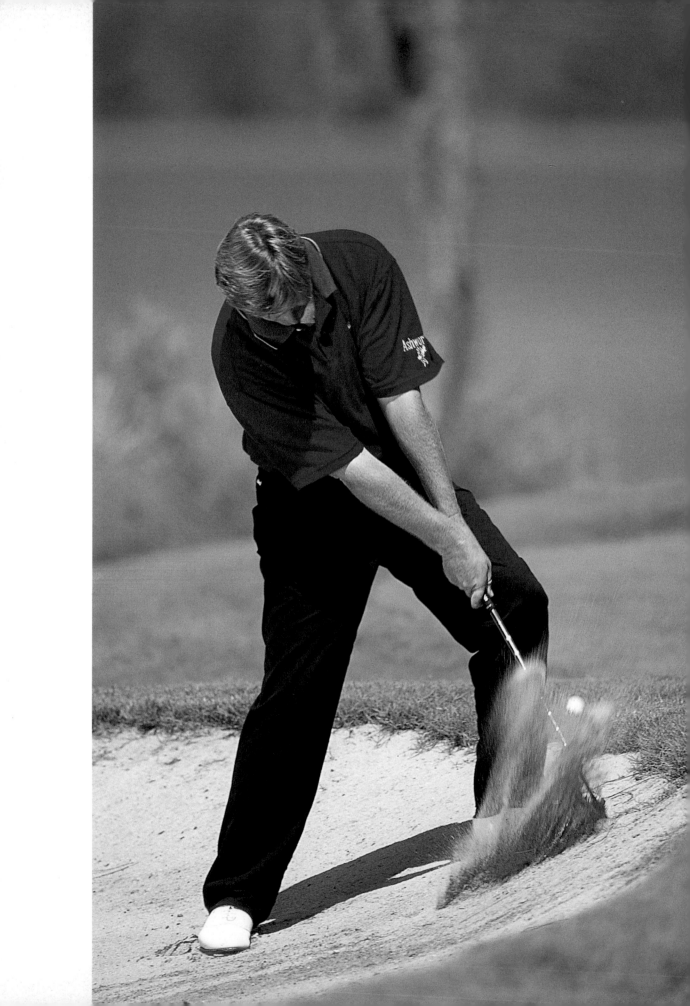

Downhill lies

CREATE A STEEP ANGLE OF ATTACK

Make no mistake, this is a real toughie. Maybe the hardest greenside bunker shot of all, in fact. A downhill lie in sand represents a multi-part problem. For one thing, playing a short shot off any kind of downslope feels terribly uncomfortable – for some reason much more so than when you're playing from an upslope lie. On top of that, it's tough to get the right sort of contact in the sand and, of course, you've a real job on your hands creating enough height on the shot.

It's not especially inviting, is it? But it's not a shot you should be frightened of. A few technical pointers should see you through. As I explained previously, on any kind of slope your weight should favour the lower foot. So, really lean on to your left side and try to get your left shoulder as low as possible. A lot of people say you need the ball back in your stance on this shot. Not me. The way I see it, you need to place the ball forward of centre to help encourage yourself to get that weight over on your left foot. That's the priority. And open the clubface so that it lays virtually flat to the sand.

Hinge your wrists early in the backswing to promote a steep angle of attack in the downswing.

Before you rush in and play the shot, take just a few extra seconds to rehearse your backswing so as to make sure the clubhead doesn't get snagged in the back lip of the bunker. The chances are you'll have to hinge your wrists a lot quicker than you would normally, so it's important to familiarise yourself with that movement.

In the backswing, keep your weight firmly planted on the lower foot and then try to swing down on a steep angle of attack. Again, identify a spot in the sand behind the ball and bury the clubhead into that spot. Stay down through impact and promise yourself you're not going to peek too soon. The ball is certain to come out low. You don't have to look to find that out.

Unlike the majority of shots around the green, you have some uncompromising course management decisions to consider, too. Going for the pin won't always be the smart play. Sometimes it won't even be possible. Basically, you should always look to land the ball in a spot where you have plenty of green to work with to allow for the extra run. If that means you can't go at the pin, then so be it. Accept that fact and just concentrate on leaving yourself a putt for your next shot. Like I say, it's a real toughie this one. But with a little practice you'll learn to deal with it.

Then release the clubhead down the slope, chasing after the ball.

Bury the clubhead in a plugged lie

In this situation, the first thing you have to understand is that it's impossible to get backspin. I certainly can't get backspin from a plugged lie and no one else can, either. It just doesn't happen. So it's vital you allow for plenty of run on the ball. Just as I explained to you in the shot from a downslope, if it's not practical to go for the flag, don't be afraid to aim for the fat of the green. The second thing is this – it's easy to leave the ball in the sand. Too easy. So be as aggressive as you like. Take it from me, there's not a great deal of finesse involved with this one.

Your set-up is, as always, pretty much make or break time. Basically you want to have everything square – from the clubface, all the way to your feet, hips and shoulders. Place the ball in the centre of your stance and nudge your hands, and your body-weight, more towards your left side than you would for a regular trap shot. Now you're looking good.

In the backswing you need to feel that you pick the club up quite steeply, hinging the wrists almost as soon as the club starts to move away from the ball. And make your backswing a long one. You must do that or you'll never be able to generate the considerable clubhead speed necessary to force the ball up and over that front lip. Now you can thump the clubhead into the sand behind the ball – and I mean really thump it. I like to think of burying the clubhead 'heel first' into the sand, because it promotes a steep, stabbing action which is exactly what I want. It's the one bunker shot where a followthrough is pretty much non-existent. You've just got to hit down and hit down hard.

If it's a really bad lie, I sometimes try to imagine I'm creating a semi-controlled explosion of sand around the ball. That helps convey the kind of positive, hard-hitting swing thoughts I need. I suggest you think along the same lines. And let me remind you again, there will be plenty of run on the ball when it lands, so allow yourself lots of green to work with.

When the ball is buried, hit the shot twice as hard as you would from a perfect lie.

Stay down when the ball is below your feet

I said earlier that 99% of all shots around the green are best played with a choked-down grip. Well, this shot represents the other 1%. Obviously, you don't want to make the club any shorter when you're struggling as it is just to reach the ball. Naturally, you want all the length the shaft can provide. So grip it full length for this one.

Your knees are the key to a well-balanced, stable address position. You really have to go for for a lot more flex than normal to help get the clubhead down to the level of the ball. This is where the 'extension' comes from, allied to a little extra bend from the waist. Also spread your feet wider apart than normal. This is yet another device to help you reach the ball and to establish a feeling of stability.

Now you're in great shape to maintain good balance in this awkward position, and that's at least half the battle. Sense that you cock your wrists abruptly in the takeaway, almost as though you're trying to point the shaft of the club straight up at the sky. You then need to concentrate doubly-hard on keeping your head at the same level throughout the downswing. In doing so you'll avoid the disastrous thin shot and also give yourself every chance of hitting the perfect spot behind the ball. Through impact, feel that you 'swing left' with a very open clubface.

A slightly more upright swing is inevitable, as is a fair degree of slice-spin, so aim even further to the left than you would for a regular bunker shot in order to allow for the ball to move from left to right, both through the air and when it hits the ground.

Make no mistake, this is a tough one, so put in some practice and don't be disheartened if your first few attempts are not a rip-roaring success.

Make a real 'wristy' swing and concentrate doubly-hard on keeping
your head at the same level throughout until the ball is well on its way.

Ball above your feet – swing with the slope

This is the sloping lie that tends to feel a lot more natural to most golfers and therefore a lot less intimidating. However, any ball above the level of your stance needs some playing and it certainly isn't as straightforward as it might seem.

The first thing you need to do is grip the club 'short' in order to bring the clubhead up to the same level as the ball. Feel as though you stand a little taller, too, with not quite so much bend from the waist. You can also see that I'm aiming right of the target – normally unheard of in a bunker – in order to allow for the ball to move right to left through the air and on landing. Remember, any shot, whether from the fairway or from the sand, is liable to generate hook-spin.

As well as aiming right of target, there's another big difference to this shot over

Stand tall, aim right, and swing the club back inside the line and behind you.

other shots from sand. Instead of taking the club back outside the line, you need to feel that you swing 'with the slope' – in other words, inside the line and thus producing a much more rounded feeling to your swing. Then come back into the sand and through on that exact same line. So in effect you're swinging on a pronounced in-to-out path, which is actually going to feel pretty natural with the ball being so far above the level of your stance.

As I've described, and as you can see in this sequence, the ball comes out left of where I'm aiming. It will also have hook-spin, so it's going to go even further left when it lands, and come out on a slightly higher trajectory, so bear that in mind also.

Sidehill lies in the sand are not the easiest shots in the world but if you adapt your set-up as I've described, and commit yourself to hitting your 'spot' in the sand, you'll cope just fine and escape every time – no problem.

Pick a spot in the sand and swing 'away from yourself' on a definite in-to-out path

DRILL: *Six balls — six different lies*

Becoming a better bunker player is not something that happens overnight, but here's a way to speed up the learning process. Place six balls in the same bunker, each one in a slightly different lie. To start, you might go for two decent lies, two uphill lies, one downhill lie and one plugged lie. That's a decent variety.

Once you're in the sand, the key is to start thinking about how the ball is going to come out and what techniques are likely to be most effective. You can't just get in there and hope for the best. It's a precise art, so assess each shot on its own merits. How high do you think the ball will fly? How far will it roll? Is it a job for your 60-degree sand-wedge or your regular sand-wedge? It seems like a lot to think about, but after you've worked at this drill a few times you'll find yourself making instinctive decisions. With this exercise, you will learn to 'read' the lie of the ball more accurately and make a better job of actually executing the shot, all of it based on experience and experimentation – the two key elements of this practice drill.

If you were to spend just one hour working on this exercise, you'd soon start to understand the actual physics of bunker play. Not only that, it actually educates you in the art of getting up and down in two, maybe even holing the occasional bunker shot. Believe me, that's not as unrealistic as you might think. Try it and see how you get on.

Clean lies: Keep the clubface open, pick a spot in the sand and swing freely.

Ball below feet: Aim left and swing left.   *Upslope: Be much more aggressive.*

Ball above feet: Aim right and swing around your body.   *Downhill lie: Expect a lower ball flight.*

The intermediate length bunker shot

Here's a killer shot. It's neither a full-length fairway bunker shot nor a greenside splash shot. It's an in-between shot, which for a lot of golfers is a recipe for misunderstanding how to play it. As I see it, the main problem is one of confusion. Lots of golfers ask themselves, 'do I play this as a bunker shot, or as a pitch shot from grass?' About 99% of those golfers fail to make up their mind. They get caught in two minds – and as soon as that happens they can kiss good-bye to a decent shot.

From the sort of range seen in this sequence – about 50 yards – this is first and foremost a bunker shot, not a pitch shot. You can't play it like a regular greenside splash shot, though. And this applies to any distance between 40 and 70 yards.

Your 56-degree sand-wedge will do the job. There's no need for any more club than that. And normal pitch shot rules apply. So that means choking down on the club one inch and adopting a *slightly* open stance.

For 40- to 70-yard bunker shots...

The key now is to take less sand than you would for a greenside bunker shot. So, if you usually aim to hit the sand two inches behind the ball, this time you need to think more in terms of half an inch. Make a tidy swing, keeping your legs and lower body pretty solid, and commit yourself to hitting that spot. You can almost forget about the ball altogether. That's not your primary focus here, the spot in the sand is. So be positive and accelerate the clubhead into that spot. There's no bail-out here. Providing you stick to the rules and trust your instincts, the ball will come out just fine.

As for getting the distance right, that's something for you to discover during practice. What I would say is that it's important you know your limits. A 56-degree sand-wedge will probably see you OK up to about 70 yards – just. Anything up to 90 yards and it's probably the same shot, only with a pitching-wedge. For distances beyond that, though, I think you need to treat this more like a pitch shot rather than a bunker shot. That means striking the ball as cleanly as possible, just as I described in the earlier chapter on pitching.

I'd suggest you use your 56-degree sand-wedge and aim to take less sand than normal.

From short range, give it a stab

Having played the long bunker shot, let's finish this chapter with the shortest shot you can ever manufacture from sand. This is a pretty advanced technique I'm about to show you, but I'd encourage every golfer to give it a go in practice and see if they can develop the skill and the confidence to consider playing it on the golf course.

This shot works best when there's virtually no distance between you and the flag, ideally when the ball is on a slight upslope in a bunker. Either that or the green slopes steeply away from you, so you need to pitch the ball on the edge of the putting surface and let it release down to the flag.

What I want you to do is set up even more open than you do for a regular bunker shot. That means laying your sand-wedge virtually flat to the sand, so much so you could almost rest a glass of water on the clubface. Also, aim your feet, hips and shoulders way left of the target. Then really flex your knees, so you're sitting down more than normal, and sense that your hands are a little lower at address.

Hinge your wrists quite abruptly as you take the club away from the ball – low hands at address encourages that – thus creating a pretty steep arc in your backswing. Try to make sure your knees stay solid and that your weight is evenly balanced. Now select your point of entry in the sand, something like two inches behind the ball, and 'stab' the clubhead down on that spot. Be positive – you should feel as though you really thump the sand with the sole of the club, almost creating a jarring sensation as the clubhead meets the sand.

Unlike most bunker shots, there isn't going to be much of a follow through with this shot. But you don't need to worry about that. As long as you pick your mark in the sand and make an 'aggressive stab', like a thumping of the sand, you'll produce the most delicate of shots. The ball will pop up

This is a great shot to have up your sleeve when you need the ball to pop up and sit down quickly. It's one that you need to practise first though.

in the air quite steeply, but won't travel far forwards, and it will land like a butterfly with sore feet. Just perfect. Like I've said, it's an ambitious shot. But with a little practice there's no reason in the world why you shouldn't be able to master it. So be bold and give it a try.

TROUBLE SHOTS

'It's fair to say that you'll have more of your share of these shots than I will, but part and parcel of becoming a better golfer is being able to deal with these difficulties. That's because many club golfers will invariably turn a tough spot into a high number. Make a few of those in a round and it soon gets costly.'

A LOT OF AMATEURS have a view that top professional golfers such as myself play flawless golf day in day out. Sure, they figure we have the odd bad hole, but they mostly assume we tee up on the first hole, hit the ball down the middle, hit the green, maybe hole a putt but certainly do no worse than two-putt, then just go ahead and repeat that process for the next 17 holes. Easy game.

Sadly, that isn't the case. I'd love to say that I always make steady progress from tee to green, hitting all the fairways and finding the middle of every green. But for the most part it just doesn't happen. We hit bad shots, just like any other human being. There are some days where I might hit only half the fairways I aim at and only just creep into double figures for greens hit in regulation.

I know amateurs find that hard to believe when they read about me winning a tournament at 10, 15 or even 20 under par. It's true, though. No golfer is a machine and it's impossible to hit every shot perfectly. For that reason, a trouble shot of some shape or form is seldom far around the corner.

In this chapter I'm going to demonstrate a few of the more common trouble shots that you might face in a round of golf. A few of them you'll recognise (possibly all too well!) and a few of them you won't. But believe me if you play this game long enough you'll face them all in time, so it's best to have not just the knowledge about how to play them, but also the experience gained from a few, well chosen minutes. So let's go. Apart from anything else, these shots are fun to try.

Slope chipping

Here's something you can't avoid, not on any golf course – sloping lies. Let me demonstrate a simple formula and straightforward technique for dealing with 'uphillers' and 'downhillers'.

USE LESS LOFT ON AN UPSLOPE...

It amazes me how often I see this shot left well short. The mistake golfers make isn't so much technique, more their club selection. They basically go with too much loft, failing to appreciate that there might be as much as 15 or 20 degrees of slope to deal with. Add that to the loft of, say a sand-wedge, and it's no wonder the ball comes up miles short of the hole. There's something like 70 degrees of effective loft coming into play. Way too much, in other words.

So don't make the same mistake. Let the upslope work in your favour. If you select a less-lofted club you can make a shorter swing, you don't have to hit the shot quite so hard, you generate less spin and consequently get a nice amount of smooth run on the ball. That all means it's far easier to judge distance.

In this instance, where the slope is quite severe, I've chosen a 7-iron. Not only does this enable me to play the shot with the simplest of techniques – it's really nothing more than an extended putting stroke – it also promotes a lowish flight and therefore plenty of run. That's good, because the sooner you can get the ball on the ground, rolling just like a putt, the better your judgement of distance is likely to be. That's a useful rule of thumb with most chips — turn the shot into a putt as early as possible.

A slightly wider stance gives you a nice solid base so you won't have a tendency to sway.

Keep wrist action to a minimum to promote a sweeping motion through impact.

That shallow angle of attack allows the loft on the club to do the work for you.

...AND MORE LOFT ON A DOWNSLOPE

When faced with the opposite shot, a chip off a downslope, it's simply a case of reversing the rules I've just explained for the uphill lie. The first thing to consider is that a downslope delofts the clubface, which is bound to result in a flatter, potentially fiery, ball-flight. So the key is to take your most lofted club to help counter the effects of the downslope as much as possible.

Having made the right club selection, the next step is setting up correctly. You have to place the ball back near the middle of your stance. Your weight is bound to be thrown forward anyway due to the nature of the slope, so don't fight that. Just concentrate on building a solid, well-balanced foundation, your weight favouring the left side. With your hands well ahead of the ball, you're all set.

Make a conscious effort to hinge your wrists a little sooner than you would for a normal chip shot and keep your weight just where you had it at address. In the downswing, sense that the clubhead follows the ball down the slope, as low to the ground as you can keep it. Don't, whatever you do, try to help the ball into the air because you will thin it, guaranteed. Like I say, if you get the clubhead chasing down the slope after the ball, you'll be OK. You'll negotiate this shot just fine.

One thing I will say as a warning, though. This is a much tougher shot than a chip from an upslope so don't be too clever. Give yourself more margin for error when picking a landing area. Be satisfied in the knowledge that your next shot should be a putt.

Hands and weight forward, ball back in stance.   *Hinge your wrists a little sooner and make a longer swing.*

Feel as though you are hitting down into impact and chasing the ball down the slope.

It's essential to stay down on this shot for as long as possible.

DRILL: *Downhill chips train a crisper strike*

Cast your mind back to earlier in the book and you'll hopefully remember the principal message that sums up the perfect set-up for a successful chipping action. *'Ball back, hands and weight forward'*, in case you'd forgotten. These set-up factors promote a tidy technique, a slightly descending angle of attack and a crisp strike – the hallmarks of a good chip shot.

Chipping from a downhill lie, while not the easiest shot in the world, is a great practice drill because it encourages all these principles of a good chipping action – ball back, hands and weight forward – and actually helps exaggerate those feelings. And when you're trying to learn something, that can only help the process.

So, try chipping a few balls off a downslope. Let me stress again, place the ball back in your stance and sense that your weight and your hands favour the left side – on a

ADVANCED TIP: *KILL THE FIRST BOUNCE*

If you're on a downslope and you don't have much green to work with, try landing the ball in the first cut of rough just short of the putting surface. It kills the speed of the shot and buys you some more space to work with. It's risky, because you're leaving the first bounce to chance, but in a calculated risk situation it's a useful option to have up your sleeve. Give the shot a try in a practice round and see how you get on.

downslope that's going to feel quite natural anyway. Try to get to the stage where you're making crisp, ball-then-turf contact. Now, go find yourself a flat lie and hit some shots, applying the same principles to your technique. Chipping will never have seemed so easy. That's great for your confidence and confidence is great for your short game.

Keep your hands 'soft' from a bare lie

I doubt if there's a more intimidating chip shot than this one, the ball sitting on a bare lie with not a blade of grass in sight. Even for me, getting up and down from here is not easy. Still, I would expect to put this one inside six feet more times than not and I don't see any reason why you shouldn't look to do that, either. Certainly in these next few sentences I can get you beyond the stage of duffing it halfway to the hole.

The first thing to stress is that if you tense up, you can kiss good-bye to an up-and-down save. If anything, I want you to feel that you actually relax your grip pressure. Hold the club as light as possible, without it actually feeling loose in your hands. This helps relax your wrists, enabling them to hinge freely as you swing the club back and forth. And that's important.

Technique-wise, it's every bit a normal chip shot. It's just that the nature of the lie means there is less margin for error. The soil around the ball in this situation was quite

Play this shot holding the club softer than you ever have before,
allowing your wrists to hinge freely in the backswing

loosely packed, almost dusty, so I actually played this a little bit like a bunker shot, keeping my hands and wrists real soft.

Most bare lies will be nothing like this, though. More likely it will be bone-hard under foot, with no 'give' at all in the ground. In such a situation you can use exactly the same technique, except you need to 'scalp' the ball cleanly off the bare surface. Put the ball an inch or so further back in your stance to help promote that clean contact. Also, leave your sand-wedge in the bag and play it with a pitching-wedge, or even a 9-iron. As you know, on a sand-wedge the leading edge is actually higher than the back edge of the sole. Off a tight lie that's obviously going to cause problems because you can't 'nip' the ball off the ground. The high leading edge means you nearly always end up thinning it. However, the pitching-wedge has a leading edge that sits tighter and flusher to the ground which makes it far more effective for getting at the bottom of the ball.

Mentally, this is a particularly difficult shot because it looks pretty intimidating. But as I say, relax, play it with soft hands and wrists and you'll soon overcome your fears.

Make an extra effort to keep your head, body and legs very still as you
swing the club down smoothly, but wih conviction.

Left-handed escape shots

I'm not faced with this shot very often, but the few
occasions in my career I've had to play it, I've been very
relieved to have it up my sleeve. I remember one particular
instance in the World Matchplay Championship, on the
18th hole on the famous West Course at Wentworth, I had
hooked my drive into bushes up the left. Without the left-
handed shot, I'd have probably had to take a penalty drop,
which is expensive at my level. The fact is, without this
shot there aren't exactly a bundle of useful alternatives. You
could try the back-handed shot, striking the ball with the
upturned toe of the club, but personally I think that's a lot
harder shot to play.

So let's concentrate on this one. At address you have to
think hard about all the things you usually take for granted.
For starters, your left hand should be below your right – a
weird sensation in itself. Stand more upright than you
would for a regular chip shot, also a little more open, and
make sure that your right arm is comfortably extended.
This is all going to feel very strange, so take a few practice
swings to familiarise yourself with the correct movement,
each time trying to get a feel for the 'low spot' in your
swing. That exact point where you feel the clubhead
naturally brushes the ground is where you need to position
the ball in your stance.

A stiff-wristed half-swing is the best way I can describe
to you the ideal technique. You just can't afford to let your
wrists hinge as much as they would in a normal swing –
that introduces too much margin for error. Basically you
need to be thinking 'all arms' and don't let your hands
travel back any further than hip height.

Accelerate the club down into the back of the ball and
try to follow through. If you keep your head nice and
steady, and don't look up too soon, you'll be surprised at
the decent contact you can make. This is no time for being
greedy, though, so just settle for getting the ball back in
play. It won't look pretty, but if you can progress it 30
yards up the fairway, you've done well. Basically by not
taking a penalty drop, you've already saved one shot. With
your ball now back in a sensible position, you can hopefully
make the most of your escape and save another stroke to
par with some good approach play.

A high-flying alternative

I'm only a few paces off line here, but unfortunately I'm right behind a small copse of trees – not an uncommon scenario on most golf courses. With only 80 yards to the flag, there's no way I can hook or slice the ball round the trees – it's simply too short a shot. And there's no real chance of playing a low punch because the overhanging branches are in my way. That leaves one option, the high-flier.

First things first, you need to go with plenty of loft. I'm using my 56-degree sand-wedge, which will just about clear the top of the tree and get me to the green. At address you need to feel that 60% of your weight is on your left foot, also that your hands are level with the ball. The ball should be just forward of centre.

In the backswing take the club straight back away from the ball and really try to feel like you make a more upright swing than usual. A pretty full one, too. This is no time for half-measures. In the downswing you can hit this shot as hard as your driver. It's fun, and you're not going to over-shoot the target in a million years, so really go for it and release the club aggressively through the ball. If you find the middle of the clubface with this one you'll get all the height in the world, so don't be tempted to lean back on your right side and help the ball into the air.

Experiment a little to see just how high you can hit the ball. Obviously you have to make sure you avoid the tree – that's the main goal – but I think you'll be surprised how much height and length you can generate with this technique.

As far as trouble shots go, this is a pretty useful one. Not only will it help you in the sort of situation you see me in here, but it is also a shot worth considering if you're pitching over a bunker to a really tight pin position.

You need to make a full, upright backswing and an aggresive swish through the ball.

Ball above feet

When the ball is this far above your feet, grip right down to the metal.

The shot you can see me playing here looks absolutely outrageous, but it's not as unlikely as you might think. OK, this ball is sitting somewhere around knee height, but if the areas around the bunkers on your home course are occupied by rough, which I find is often the case, this type of thing can happen. Even if it doesn't get quite this severe, and the ball sits only half this distance above your feet, the principles I'm about to explain will stand you in good stead.

The secret to playing this chip shot well, as you can see from this photograph *(left)*, is to grip the club right down to the metal on the shaft. That means you can at least stand fairly normally to the ball, without having to make ridiculous adjustments to your set-up. The only other thing you must do is aim way right, because on a slope such as this it feels like you could almost hit the ball over your left shoulder.

In the swing itself, you want minimum upper-body movement. It's virtually all hands-and-wrists. So keep everything pretty steady from the waist up and simply feel like you move the club back and through with a smooth, hands-and-arms swing. It's almost like a wristy 'jab' – that's probably the best way I can describe to you the ideal movement. Certainly that's how it feels. As I explained in the set-up, you can expect the ball to pop out miles left of where you're aiming, not a problem if you're aiming miles right!

Set up a few balls above the level of your feet at your home course and give this chip shot a try. Even if the slope isn't as severe as the one you see me on here, you still need to grip well down the shaft and make a wristy type swing, keeping your head rock steady.

Apart from the obvious benefits to your game, creating these shots and learning how to play them is great experience and great fun. It encourages a lively imagination and when it comes to the short game, that's one of the biggest assets you can possess.

Make a wristy backswing.

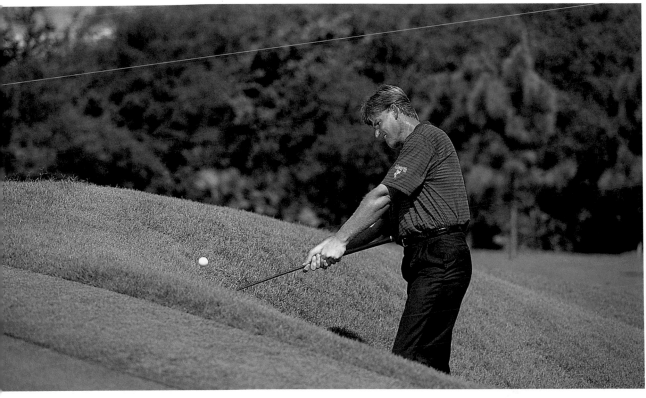

Keep body movement to a minimum and make a hands-and-arms swing into impact.

Be firm and allow for the ball to come out way left.

Ball below feet

Another real toughie, this one. The ball is well below the level of my stance, so much so that it's a real struggle just reaching down to it – a problem not helped by the fact that I'm 6ft 3in tall. As with the previous shot this is the sort of thing that can happen around the edges of bunkers, where steep banking is an obvious feature, and on American-style courses where dramatic mounding is so often a part of the greenside protection system.

Once again let me stress that although this is a severe example, the principles I'm explaining are just as relevant on slopes far more subtle than this one.

Any time you're in a situation where the ground is falling away from you is a good time to think about using more loft. In this instance, you can make that maximum loft – a 60-degree sand-wedge if you're sensible enough to carry one. If you don't already have one of these clubs, you really should buy one. I couldn't be without a 60-degree wedge – I use it that often. Once you get one in your bag I'm sure you'll find yourself thinking the same thing.

Your address position here is really just a battle to get as comfortable and as well balanced as possible. Lean heavily on to your left leg and put plenty of flex in that right knee. Keep your spine fairly upright to stop yourself toppling forwards over the ball. That's about as good as you can probably do. Now you at least have a solid base from which to make a swing.

As you make your backswing you need to work really hard at keeping your head and upper body at the same level, because the natural tendency as you swing the club up is to let yourself be lifted up with it. You can't afford to let that happen – if you do you're going to thin the shot and the ball will travel like a bullet across the green.

Providing you stay down on the shot and keep your weight just where you set it at address, you'll make proper contact and thus generate the necessary height and distance to find the green. There's bound to be a fair bit of run on the ball, so make sure you allow for it. All in all, if you can put this shot inside 10 feet you should give yourself a big pat on the back. That's a good escape.

THE PROFESSIONAL APPROACH

'As every professional will tell you, there's a whole world of difference between looking good on the range and shooting a good score on the course. Swinging smoothly and striking the ball crisply is all very well when there's a bucket of balls by your side, but it's all different when the gun goes.'

SOME GOLFERS TAKE THEIR GAME to the course better than others. I'm sure you know guys at your home club who are just the same. The ones who look the part seem to swing the club quite nicely and hit the ball consistently enough. And yet there's something missing – they just can't produce the goods when they've a scorecard in their back pocket. Likewise, there are golfers who don't look particularly special and yet who know how to make a score happen. They just 'have the knack'. It's a tough thing to put your finger on, but it happens everywhere.

This is true at any level and it certainly happens on tour. If you were to visit a professional tournament anywhere around the world and walk along the line of players on the practice ground, you'd see a bunch of guys all striking the ball 'flush'. There really is very little difference. Look at the list of scores at the end of the day and you'd see some difference for sure. Probably a 15 shot swing from the lowest to the highest score.

This can be put down to a number of factors, many of them short-game related, others more than simply skin deep. Let me talk you through a few professional 'secrets' that I'm sure will help bring you closer to reaching your goals. These apply to every one of you, whether your target is breaking 100, 90, 80 or the magic 70.

Find your favourite pitching zone

This is surely one of the most effective strategies in the whole game of golf. It is also one of the simplest and least practised. In fact, if as many as 5% of club golfers said to me this was part of their game plan I'd be surprised. All it involves is discovering what distance you feel most comfortable pitching from. You probably have a rough idea already, but in a sub-conscious kind of way that doesn't enable you to actually capitalise on it.

As I've said, it's easy to do. Just find a quiet spot on the course during a practice round and hit half-a-dozen balls from a variety of distances between 60 and 100 yards. You could in fact do this at the driving range if you prefer. Have a couple of wedges to hand and chop and change between them. I honestly think that within 15 minutes you'll have a fair idea of what your favourite distance is. And within half-an-hour you'll know

Make an effort to discover what your favourite distance is to pitch from...

for certain. When you've made your decision, spend the next 20 minutes or so practising solely that shot and thus building your confidence level.

Then when you're on the course, tailor your game plan to involve as many of your favourite pitch shots as possible. You can even run through each hole in your mind as you drive to the golf course. On short par-4s, take the club off the tee that puts you in your 'pitching zone', from where you'll feel like you can really attack the flag for birdie. On par-5s that are out of reach in two, try to play your lay-up shot again into your 'pitching zone'. Not only is this strategy making your next shot easier, it also benefits the actual shot you're hitting because it means you probably won't feel the need to push for distance. It sharpens your focus and means you're more in control. This is called playing to your strengths. The professionals do it all the time. So should you.

because once you know that, your increased confidence will result in a more positive swing.

Learn damage limitation

I've shown you how to play some pretty fancy trouble shots in this book, but there's a flip side to that coin. It's a skill that I would describe as 'damage limitation'. By that I mean, knowing how to avoid a big number when you're in trouble. There are several factors that determine how good you are at damage limitation.

First, you need to have an honest awareness of your own personal abilities. And I mean really honest. Every time you find yourself in trouble, you need to ask yourself a few questions. What are the chances of actually executing the shot successfully? Fifty-fifty? Or less than that? Only you can ultimately decide, but I would say that if the odds are anything less than 75% in your favour you should be looking for a more realistic alternative.

You also need to assess the overall risks involved. In other words, what can you gain and what can you lose? For instance, if going for a certain recovery shot that will save you one stroke to par if it comes off, but cost you three if it doesn't, then I think that's a gamble you shouldn't be taking. It's probably wiser to chip out sideways or take a penalty drop.

As I've said, certain decisions you make on a golf course are as important as the swings themselves. My feeling is that the first priority in any spot of trouble is to get the ball back in play. That only ever costs you one shot, whereas attempting fancy recoveries can cost you a whole lot more. I'm not saying don't take a gamble – I wouldn't be showing you some of these recovery shots in this chapter if I thought that. But just be honest with yourself. Be totally realistic, not overly optimistic.

One final rule of thumb. Never attempt a recovery shot in a competition that you haven't tried in practice. The monthly medal is no time to go stepping into the unknown.

Whenever you're in a tight spot, don't rush in. Step back, count to 10, and think again.

Think first before you practise

If you're like the majority of amateurs, you probably prefer to play a few holes rather than practise. If you knew how to practise, though, I reckon you'd soon change your opinions. Practice can be fun, and seriously good for your golf, if you know how.

The first key to a good practice session is knowing what you want to work on. Don't just turn up, pull out a club and aimlessly hit balls at a variety of targets. That's going to do you no good whatsoever, because you're unlikely to be actually thinking about what you're doing. So think first. There's never a bad time to check your fundamentals and the practice green or practice ground is the place to do that. Check your grip, lay clubs on the ground to check your alignment and make sure your posture is as good as you can possibly make it. These are the things you have to rely on during a round and the more you practise them the greater the chance that they'll become second nature.

If you're practising your short game, as I am here *(see below)*, have all your clubs to hand and plenty of balls by your side. Make sure you vary your targets and vary the clubs you use. Now's the time to learn about what club does what job best. It's amazing how quickly you start to develop a picture in your mind, and a feeling in your hands, of the variety of shots you can play around the greens.

Every now and then, rather than playing a few casual holes with a friend, have a practise session together. Compete against one another – the opportunities in the short game are endless – and have the odd wager. Make it competitive, varied and fun. You'll probably get more out of an hour doing this than you would two hours on the course.

Fun shots help fire your imagination

Having fun is an important part of any learning process. Golf is no exception. That's why I recommend you experiment with wild and wacky shots every now and then. For one thing, it spices up the occasional practice session. And aside from that, it gives you a good feel for what you can and can't do with the golf ball. It also helps promote a lively imagination – gets you more used to visualising shots – and that's an asset to any golfer's short game.

You can see here I've put the ball on a steep slope in a bunker and I'm swinging back up the slope. Phil Mickelson can actually hit this shot over his head and towards the flag,

which takes some doing I can tell you. In this case I got the ball to travel literally straight up in the air like a sky-rocket.

OK, so you wouldn't try a stunt like this in a tournament, but don't let that stop you experimenting with shots like this. It really gives you an acute awareness of what your hands and the clubhead are doing in the swing. And it's even more fun if you have a few friends around to compete against. Try to invent shots between yourselves. Through trial and error, you'll probably come across a few recovery shots that you never knew you could play and might therefore consider using in a round of golf.

This sort of thing is great fun, either on your own or with a few friends. It also teaches you skills that can be a great asset to your short game.

Go head-to-head with yourself

This game isn't a new idea but I think it's a terrific way to sharpen your short game skills if you're dead-set on playing a round of golf on your own. Hit one drive on each hole and, when you get to around 100-yards or less, drop another ball on the ground. Now play two different types of approach shot with two different clubs.

Try to vary the shots as much as possible and never use the same club twice on the same hole. Vary the trajectory of the shots, pitch one short and one on the green, try to play one shot with spin and one without, keep experimenting all the time.

Carry on like this for however many holes you intend playing. Whether that's six holes, nine, or the full 18, it's a great way to hone your competitive edge and sharpen your short game skills. The more creative you are in your practice sessions, the more effective you'll be on the golf course. And that's true for every single department of the short game that I've shown you in this book.

Drop two balls down and try to vary the shots as much as possible.

'The single quickest way to start shooting lower scores at your home course is to improve your short game. I know you've probably heard that before, but hopefully coming from me it might hit home a little harder, because believe me it is so true. Through the pages of this book I've given you all the know-how that you need in order to develop a better short game. It's up to you now. With some regular practice, you will lower your handicap – guaranteed. Even as little as one hour a week will make a bigger difference than you ever imagined. Make your next practice session a short game session. You won't look back. I'm certain of that.'